ISOBEL ARMSTRONG
General Editor

BRYAN LOUGHREY
Advisory Editor

James Joyce

JAMES JOYCE
from a portrait of 1935 by JACQUES-EMILE BLANCHE
National Portrait Gallery, London

James Joyce

Steven Connor

Northcote House

in association with
The British Council

© Copyright 1996 by Steven Connor

First published in 1996 by Northcote House Publishers Ltd, Plymbridge House,
Estover Road, Plymouth PL6 7PY, United Kingdom.
Tel: +44 (0) 1752 202368. Fax: +44 (0) 1752 202330.

British Library Cataloguing-in-Publication Data
A catalogue record for this book is available from the British Library

ISBN 0 7463 0753 5

Typeset by Florencetype Ltd, Tiverton
Printed and bound in the United Kingdom

Contents

Biographical Outline

1882	2 February. Born in Dublin.
1888	Enrolled at Clongowes Wood College.
1891	Withdrawn from Clongowes as family finances worsen.
1893–8	Attends Belvedere College.
1898–1902	Attends University College Dublin.
1900	Writes an Ibsenite play *A Brilliant Career*, now lost; publishes 'Ibsen's New Drama', in the *Fortnightly Review*; begins writing series of prose sketches, or 'epiphanies'.
1901	Private publication of *The Day of the Rabblement*.
1902	December. Leaves for Paris, brief enrolment in medical school.
1903	April. Return to Dublin.
	13 August. Death of mother.
1904	Verse satire on Dublin literary life, *The Holy Office*, privately printed; essay, 'A Portrait of the Artist', rejected by *Dana*; at work on *Dubliners* and *Stephen Hero*.
	16 June. First date with Nora Barnacle, adopted as the date of the action of *Ulysses*.
	8 October. Joyce and Nora leave Dublin together for Pola in Austria; Joyce teaches English.
1905	Move to Trieste.
	27 July. First son, Giorgio, born.
	First version of *Dubliners* completed and sent to Grant Richards.
1906–7	Bank clerk in Rome; conceives *Ulysses* as short story.

1907	Return to Trieste.
	26 July. Birth of daughter, Lucia.
	Publication of volume of poems, *Chamber Music*; writes 'The Dead'.
1907–8?	Abandons long autobiographical novel *Stephen Hero*, and begins recasting it as *A Portrait of the Artist as a Young Man*.
1909	August and October–December. Two visits to Dublin, shocked by claim of a friend, Vincent Cosgrave, that he had an affair with Nora in 1904.
	20 December. Joyce and partners open the first cinema in Dublin, the *Volta*.
1912	July–September. Joyce's last visit to Ireland; satirical parting poem, *Gas from a Burner*.
1914	*A Portrain of the Artist as a Young Man* begins serial publication in the *Egoist*; *Dubliners* finally published; *Ulysses* begun; *Giacomo Joyce* written.
1915	Moves to Zurich.
1916	*A Portrait of the Artist as a Young Man* published.
1917	Beginning of serious eye troubles; Harriet Weaver begins lifelong patronage of Joyce family.
1918	*Exiles* published; serial publication of *Ulysses* begins in the *Little Review*.
1919	Return to Trieste.
1920	Move to Paris; suspension of *Ulysses* publication in the *Little Review* for legal reasons.
1922	2 February. Publication of *Ulysses* on Joyce's fortieth birthday.
1922	October. Begins notes for *Finnegans Wake*.
1924	First section of *Finnegans Wake*, known until publication as *Work in Progress*, published in *Transatlantic Review*.
1927	April–November. Book I of *Finnegans Wake* appears in *transition*; publication of second volume of verse, *Pomes Penyeach*.
1929	November. Publication of *Work in Progress* suspended; publication of volume of essays about the work by Samuel Beckett and others, *Our Exagmination Round His Factification for Incamination of Work in Progress*.

1928   Much of book III of *Finnegans Wake* composed.
1929–32   Intensifying mental illness of daughter, Lucia.
1931   Marriage to Nora Barnacle; publication of Stuart Gilbert's *James Joyce's 'Ulysses'*.
1932   Death of father.
1934   US publication of *Ulysses* after successful defence against charges of obscenity.
1934   Publication of Frank Budgen's *James Joyce and the Making of 'Ulysses'*.
1939   9 May. Publication of *Finnegans Wake*; Joyces flee Paris for Zurich.
1941   13 January. Joyce dies during an eye operation in Zurich at age 58.

Abbreviations

D.   *Dubliners*, ed. Hans Walter Gabler and Walter Hettche (New York and London: Garland, 1993)

FW   *Finnegans Wake* (London: Faber & Faber, 1958) (references are to page and line numbers)

L.   *Letters of James Joyce*, 3 vols., vol. i, ed. Stuart Gilbert (London: Faber & Faber 1957); vols. ii and iii, ed. Richard Ellmann (London: Faber & Faber 1966)

P.   *A Portrait of the Artist as a Young Man*, ed. Hans Walter Gabler and Walter Hettche (New York and London: Garland, 1993)

SH   *Stephen Hero*, ed. Theodore Spencer (London: Jonathan Cape, 1969)

U.   *Ulysses: The Corrected Text*, ed. Hans Walter Gabler with Wolfhard Steppe and Claus Melchoir (Student's Edition; Harmondsworth: Penguin, 1986) (this edition is set from the Garland edition referred to in the Select Bibliography; references are to page, episode, and line numbers)

1

Introduction: The Workings of Work

James Joyce wrote four significant books: a volume of short stories, a highly worked fictional autobiography, a novel which for many is still to be regarded as the most remarkable ever written, and a brilliant, innovative, but scarcely describable exercise in word-invention and decomposition. In addition there is a play, which it would be fair to say has never exactly established itself in the theatre ('Meet Flanagan. He's working on a dramatization of *Exiles*', goes the old Dublin joke); a few dozen frail lyrics ingeniously but uncompellingly praised by Joyce's brother Stanislaus as 'songs without thoughts',[1] which perhaps only the most hopelessly addicted Joycians can read with any serious attention; a fantasy memoir; a smattering of critical essays, mostly written in Joyce's penurious youth (not that Joyce ever became significantly less penurious, but his time became too precious for such things later in his life); an abundance of letters, a number of satirical squibs, and a series of brilliant limericks. In terms of published output, James Joyce is far from prodigious.

But if in this, narrowly quantitative, sense Joyce is not much of an author, there is another, more important, sense in which he may be vastly more than one. For may it not be that Joyce is the author not just of the handful of texts credited to him, but also of all the work produced in his name? Michel Foucault coined the term 'founder of discursivity' to describe this kind of authorship. Such authors

> are unique in that they are not just the authors of their own works. They have produced something else: the possibilities and the rules for the formation of other texts. ... Freud is not just the author of *The Interpretation of Dreams* or *Jokes and their Relation to the Unconscious*;

> Marx is not just the author of the *Communist Manifesto* or *Capital*: they both have established an endless possibility of discourse.[2]

'James Joyce' indeed now names a peripatetic global institution, a whole hermeneutic culture, a vast and ever-expanding enterprise of exposition and interpretation. The 'work of Joyce' is more than just a particular collection of texts; it is a generative code, a discursive epidemic, a chain letter. To write about Joyce's work, to add another act of reading to this immense unfolding, is a humbling, exhilarating, intimidating thing. Inevitably, any such reading will be given, consciously or unconsciously, to reflect on the nature and implications of the extravagance (literally *extra-vagari*, to wander outside), at once amicable and appetitive, of Joycian reading and writing, a writing that seems so strangely and stubbornly to resist reduction to an *œuvre*, or mere 'body of work'. We are going to see that it is a form of writing which in fact fundamentally explores and redefines the meaning of 'work' itself.

Joyce is a modernist, not only because of the specific kinds of experiment, innovation, or challenge that his writing offers to literary and artistic tradition, but also because of the particular conditions under which that work is produced. Joyce's modernism, like that of many of his contemporaries, is defined by a refusal of the quotidian world of work, and the assertion of the sanctity of the work of art against the vulgar products of mere employment. Joyce was the eldest son in a large family and grew up in the relative economic security of the property-owning middle class. He enjoyed an education at the three most prestigious educational institutions in Catholic Ireland, all of them run by the Jesuit order: Clongowes Wood College, Belvedere College, and University College Dublin. By the time he had become an undergraduate, his family, hitherto comfortably well off, despite its proliferating children, had entered a period of great financial insecurity, partly due to the unreliability of his father, John Joyce.

Joyce became a modernist at the point when he made a choice to become an artist in distinction to a more secure middle-class occupation. For Joyce, to be an artist was to refuse the market place and to embrace the nomadic, insecure, and, as it seemed to many, parasitic life of the bohemian. We are apt to forget how recent an invention the figure of the bohemian artist is in European cultures. It does not date back much further than the late eighteenth and early nineteenth centuries, a period during which the collapse of the system of patronage, and the erosion of the privilege accorded to the writer, painter, and musician, who was now required to earn his living much like everybody else, began to make the work of the artist appear anomalous at best and superfluous at worst. Artists had no choice but to accept their reduced role, and to hug and nurture the very principles of their marginality. Henceforth, to be an artist was to withdraw from the world of getting and spending, to refuse to participate in the economic processes which began to encroach on every area of social life. This refusal expressed itself in a deepening mistrust of a society organized more and more around the logic of the commodity, the production of objects the value of which is determined wholly by the vicissitudes and vagaries of economic exchange in the market place.

In fact, the marginalization of the artist from the eighteenth century onwards managed to achieve something that centuries of aesthetic and critical enquiry had conspicuously failed to do: it threw up a universally applicable definition of art, now characterized clearly as the *opposite of work*. All over the newly industrializing world, bourgeois families trembled with the unspoken dread that young Henry (or, worse still, Henrietta) might one day announce the intention of going in for art, compared with which prospect a career as a streetwalker or receiver of stolen goods seemed like honest toil. But it is perhaps not often enough noticed that the hardening of definitions of art, the artist, and the aesthetic took place in close parallel to the steady moralization of work from the eighteenth century onwards, and the deepening from the late eighteenth century onwards of the association between occupation and identity, the nature of one's labour and the nature of one's being. For Marx, the scandal of wage-slavery is to be measured, not in terms of the quantitative burden of labour it imposes, but in its denial of that ideal of authentic labour by which means alone man can fulfil his nature. The moralization of work can be found in scientific writings, too, in the obsession with turning energy into useful work to be found in the new science of thermodynamics, as well as in the horrifying prospect opened up by Lord Kelvin's Second Law of

Thermodynamics, which predicted the inevitable decline of the universe into the idleness of dissipated energy. Just as sociologists and political scientists drew their understanding of the meaning of social work from aesthetic ideas and from the ideal, though in practice disdained, figure of the artist, so artists and aesthetic thinkers defined themselves by negative reference to the world of work. To be an artist was to refuse (and, usually, to be refused) the idea of paid labour, but it was also, necessarily, to mimic, even to underline, the general moralization of work. The opposite of work (art) was not non-work, but a superior, redeemed, more essentially laborious kind of work.

Faced with a logic of the commodity which tended to relegate the production of art as useless, inefficient, or infantile, artists had two, sometimes associated, responses. One was to compensate for the social undervaluation of art by a massive overvaluation. Art, writers like Shelley proclaimed, spoke a higher kind of truth, and possessed a transcendent value that could not even be measured in conventional economic terms. For this tradition, which extends through Flaubert and Wilde to Joyce, the artist is a superior kind of craftsman, whose godlike labour produces the only real value in a world of degraded mass consumption. To borrow the pun which Joyce enjoyed so much in *Ulysses* that he filched it back from himself in *Finnegans Wake*, the work of art is seen as a 'massproduct' (*U.* 553. 17. 369; *FW* 546. 15), a sacramental transubstantiation of the grossly material world of mass-produced commodities.

However, the extraordinary capacity of the market to assimilate and capitalize upon the most radical challenges to its logic, and its ravening hunger to reduce works of art to the condition of commodities, also led some artists to a suspicion of the idea of the 'work' itself. Hence another, more extreme response to the social discrediting of art was for the artist to undervalue the work of art, or to refrain as far as was decently possible from producing works of art at all. Attention was thus deflected defensively from the vulnerable work of art to its less easily commodified producer. For this alternative avant-garde tradition, which ran parallel to the artist-as-craftsman tradition and which was to erupt into the pyrotechnic nihilism of Dada in the early twentieth century, the order of priority between artist and work was coolly inverted. The point of being an artist was no longer to be a supplier of goods. If it was tediously necessary to turn in the occasional piece of work, this was only to prove that one was an artist, the work itself being incidental to the artistic life of which it was the precipitate. As such, it was desirable to produce *as little as possible*. Artistic and material success became mutually defining opposites. Thus, when Samuel Beckett declared in 1945 that 'to be an artist is to fail as no other dare fail', he was both reacting against the assurance of modernist ideas of the superiority of the artist's vocation and giving voice to what had become a traditional association between being an artist and worldly failure.[3]

In fact, these two responses – artistic rivalry towards the world of work, and artistic refusal of it – are closely woven together. Both are present in the work of Gustave Flaubert, for example, whose abhorrence of small-minded bourgeois values and sensibilities and superior evaluation of the sacred vocation of the artist goes along with a curious introjection of the Puritan values of self-denying labour. This kind of ambivalence is to be seen particularly in writers of fiction or drama, since these are forms which come to be so entangled with the mass market, in all its threat and allure. Joyce inherits this complex and contradictory pattern of rivalry between the world and the artist; but his work also pushes further than any other writer or artist before him in examining and transforming their relationship. In *Dubliners* and *A Portrait of the Artist as a Young Man*, we see the attempt to embody in positive form the transfigured work which the modernist artist staked against the actual world of work; here the literary work is meant in Flaubertian manner to body forth an alternative to the corruption and narrowness of life that is its subject. In *Ulysses*, which is actually built around the contrast between two characters who represent the world of work and the world of the artist, the labour of refusal involves a much more complex and ironic engagement with the socio-economics of work. The resulting work is no longer the precipitate of a labour conceived of as wholly different in kind or removed from the real worlds of work, and the work of writing *Ulysses* is interwoven with the forms of socially organized work shown through its length. *Finnegans Wake* at once confirms the ineradicable split between the modernist work and work in modernity, and throws all the conventional distinctions between work and life into turmoil. In the very extremity of its secession both from the values of the literary market place and from the values of seriousness, integrity, and interpretability attaching to the modernist work, *Finnegans Wake* anticipates some of the transfigurations in the idea of work that have characterized the decades in which it has itself been subject to reading, and has worked to disrupt the nature of that process of reading and being read.

2

The Indefinite Article: *Dubliners*

Dubliners; not *The Dubliners*. Yet teachers and proof-readers will know that readers of this collection of stories suffer from an irresistible compulsion to supply the definite article that Joyce withholds. The desire to turn *Dubliners* into *The Dubliners* may be partly an effect of the desire to see Joyce's works as a complete organic sequence, and therefore to read back the future of his work into its beginnings. Joyce himself looked to such organic metaphors when describing the structure of his works. He pointed out that the sequence of stories in *Dubliners* followed through the stages of growth of a single person, from childhood, through adolescence, and into public life (*L*. ii. 111, 134). *A Portrait of the Artist as a Young Man* follows through the same movement; it is a *Künstlerroman*, that particular species of the *Bildungsroman*, or novel of growth and education, which deals specifically with the growth of an artist. Joyce's great technical discovery between *Stephen Hero*, the first, abandoned version of the novel, and its rewriting as *A Portrait of the Artist as a Young Man* was that growth could be the governing principle of the style as well as the principal theme of a work. Thus the growth of the artist into self-consciousness and self-command is paralleled by the gathering of the writing into the condition of a 'work'. Despite the apparent impediment to the idea of growth imposed by the restriction of the action of *Ulysses* to a single day in June 1904, Joyce was at pains to build up a structure which relates the unfolding of human history to the progress of individual human lives, most obviously perhaps in the episode known as 'The Oxen of the Sun', in which the evolution of English literary style is set in parallel with the gestation of a foetus. Whatever else it is, *Finnegans Wake* must also be seen as a massive filling-out of this analogy between ontogeny and phylogeny, the growth of the species and the growth of the individual, the macro and the micro, the all and the one.

Given this, it is understandable that readers have wanted to extend the genetic analogy in order to find the principle of organic growth operating between Joyce's works as well as within them. It seems, somehow, more than appropriate to see the sequence of texts from *Dubliners* through to *Finnegans Wake* as the working-through of a continuous set of preoccupations. Read as the definitive beginning of a life's work, *Dubliners* can be seen, not merely as the source from which that work germinates, but also as a kind of homunculus, or miniaturized version of the whole. Thus, it is almost as though the cast of characters, situations, and settings in these stories provided an ensemble of possibilities of which the later work is an actualization; as though *Dubliners* included that later work in its frame. According to this bizarre logic, the *Dubliners* collection no longer seems like a series of sketches, swiftly snatched and sparsely detailed, but comes to resemble the later work in its scope, finish, and self-possession. Reading backwards from the huge work of exegesis expended on *Ulysses* and *Finnegans Wake*, critical commentary on the stories over the years has come to emphasize more and more their qualities of symbolism and artifice, finding in them the same themes and elaborate techniques of patterning as are to be developed in the later work. And yet, of course, had Joyce never written or published anything else after *Dubliners*, it would be very unlikely that such a critical view of them could ever have been developed. In fact, even the reader who comes to these stories after making the acquaintance of the densely textured and demanding later works, is likely to find their reserve, indefiniteness, and obliquity disconcerting. The reader looking to find 'The' *Dubliners* finds only a collection of impressions; sketches rather than symbolic structures, snatched rather than contrived, dependent apparently as much upon chance as upon artistic design. The title echoes those of many other collections of short stories of the 1890s, and the early years of the new century, when there was a vogue for texts which evoked the fugitive and fragmentary moods and impressions of modern life, often with titles that testified to the looseness of their organization, and evoked the sketch

or musical impromptu rather than the masterwork: George
Egerton produced a series of such volumes, including *Keynotes*
(1893), *Discords* (1894), *Fantasias* (1898); and *Dubliners* itself
evolved out of a series of prose sketches that Joyce called
Silhouettes. The suppression – or is more simply, more neutrally,
the absence? – of the definite article in Joyce's title thus seems
appropriate to convey the indefiniteness of the events in the
stories and of the connections between them. The pressure to
make sense of the stories, to read them as unified in intention
and design, as worked over rather than emptied out, is a pressure to supply that missing article, to construe *Dubliners* as *The
Dubliners*. To borrow the handy pun proposed by Richard Pearce,
it represents a desire to turn a work which is peppered with
'holes' into a significant and inclusive 'whole'.[1] The titles of the
individual stories themselves appear to oscillate between these
alternatives, balancing the specificity of '*The* Sisters', 'After *the*
Race', '*The* Boarding House', and, most particularly, '*The* Dead'
with the obliquity of titles with either the indefinite article – '*An*
Encounter', '*A* Little Cloud', '*A* Painful Case', '*A* Mother' – or
no article at all – 'Two Gallants', 'Counterparts', 'Clay', 'Grace'.
This oscillation is a feature of the stories themselves, which can
move their reader not only in the conventional direction – from
the use of the indefinite article to the use of the definite, as characters, objects, and events become familiar in the course of the
narrative – but also in the opposite direction. Thus, as Richard
Pearce notes, the housemaid who is being conned by Corley in
'Two Gallants', and with whom we have become sufficiently
familiar for her to be called 'the woman', appears at the climactic
moment of the story through the front door of the house where
she works designated simply as 'a woman'.[2] This preference for
the indefinite is evident throughout *Dubliners* and indeed perhaps
survives into Joyce's strongly negative reaction to the (strange)
title proposed for a German translation of the book in 1927, *So
Sind Sie in Dublin* (*How They Are in Dublin*). Joyce first of all
suggested that his perspective would be better represented by
the more inclusive *So Sind Wir in Dublin* (*How We Are in Dublin*),
and then, remarking that 'I like neither', he suggested the non-
committal substitution of the place for its inhabitants with the
titles *In Dublin Stadt* (*In Dublin City*) or *Dublin an der Liffey* (*Dublin
on the Liffey*) (L. iii. 164).

9

Joyce's announcement that *Dubliners* was arranged in a sequence that was meant to follow through the stages of a single human life suggests that he wanted his book to be read as a kind of collective biography, whose subject, though it is nowhere explicitly identified in the stories themselves, would be the human population of Dublin as a whole. Joyce wrote to Constantine Curran in 1904 that he was writing a series of what he called 'epicleti' – which were to be called '"Dubliners" to betray the soul of that hemiplegia or paralysis which many consider a city' (*L*. i. 55). As many have noted, the stories are indeed thronged with examples of paralysis, physical, moral, and spiritual. The first story in the collection, 'The Sisters', focuses on the symbolic paralysis of a priest, and the last includes Gabriel Conroy's comic, and perhaps allegorical, story about Patrick Morkan's horse; the horse who had spent years walking round in circles to power a treadmill in Patrick Morkan's factory is taken out for a drive, but gets no further than the statue of William II on College Green, which he starts to orbit. Thus the collection appears to be balanced between the two great constraining forces of Irish life in the early twentieth century – the Catholic Church and the Protestant British state. Between these two alternatives, we read repeatedly of the narrow, thwarted lives of the inhabitants of Dublin, kept in their places by poverty, ignorance, fantasy, and selfishness. Many of the stories represent attempts at escape, from the day taken off school in 'An Encounter', the trip to the exotically named bazaar in 'Araby', a young girl's dream of eloping with her lover in 'Eveline', through to the drunken sprees of 'After the Race' and 'Counterparts', and the prospect of religious renewal in 'Grace'. But all of these attempts at escape round back into constriction or defeat; the boys in 'An Encounter' meet a 'queer old josser', whose sexually obsessed discourse imprisons him just as effectively as Patrick Morkan's horse; the bazaar in 'Araby' turns out to be a seedy disappointment; Eveline, in the story that bears her name, is unable to make the decision to board the ship that will carry her away from Dublin (and some readers have suspected that it is not likely to get her much further than Liverpool anyway); Farrington's drunken evening in 'Counterparts' leaves his pocket empty and him full of rage which he discharges violently upon his son; and the religious renewal in 'Grace' turns out to be hypocritical and self-serving. Joyce hints at rather than openly asserts the lesson of Dublin's paralysis, but the hints are nevertheless insistent.

It took Joyce some years to get these *Dubliners* published, mostly because of his intransigent refusal to alter or soften details which publishers thought would be disagreeable to their readers. Joyce's obstinacy on this point is admirable, if also slightly puzzling to a modern reader, since his grandiose statements of moral purpose and moral effect seem somewhat exorbitant in relation to the elliptical and understated stories to which they refer. Joyce's letter of 1906 to his publisher Grant Richards makes it clear that his stories are intended to work both as reflection of the moral corruption of Dublin and as a call to Dublin to make its soul:

> The points on which I have not yielded are the points which rivet the book together. If I eliminate them what becomes of the chapter of the moral history of my country? I fight to retain them because I believe that in composing my chapter of moral history in exactly the way I have composed it, I have taken the first step towards the spiritual liberation of my country. (*L.* i. 62–3)

In calling for spiritual liberation, Joyce saw himself as following the example of Henrik Ibsen, the Norwegian writer whom he had first encountered as an undergraduate in University College Dublin. For Ibsen too, selfhood was seen not as a mere given, but as a responsibility, a task, and a vocation; Ibsen's heroes are measured against the ideal of strenuous self-making. The point of revealing the constriction of soul of Dublin life is not merely to condemn it satirically, but to call that collective soul or resolute self-awareness reactively into being.

Central to this ethic of self-making are the ideas about the nature of art which Joyce developed early in his writing career. From about 1901, Joyce had been at work on a series of short prose sketches, which he called 'epiphanies' and which were intended to embody sudden moments of illumination or disclosure. The theory of epiphany is given its fullest exposition in fictional form in *Stephen Hero*, the first version of the autobiographical novel which Joyce abandoned to write *A Portrait of the Artist as a Young Man*. There we are told that:

> By an epiphany he meant a sudden spiritual manifestation, whether in the vulgarity of speech or of gesture or in a memorable phase of the mind itself. He believed that it was for the man of letters to record these epiphanies with extreme care, seeing that they themselves are the most delicate and evanescent of moments. (*SH* 188)

Joyce set himself diligently to the recording of scenes and snatches of conversation; Oliver St John Gogarty recorded his irritation at Joyce's habit of slipping into the lavatories of pubs to record his friends' injudicious utterances.[3] However, this account of epiphany in *Stephen Hero* is not complete, and indeed is somewhat misleading on its own. A moment later, in his exposition to his friend Cranly, Stephen describes the process of perception which is necessary and even prior to the act of recording. He takes the appearance of the clock on the Ballast Office as an example:

> I will pass it time after time, allude to it, refer to it, catch a glimpse of it. It is only an item in the catalogue of Dublin's street furniture. Then all at once I see it and know at once what it is: epiphany. . . . Imagine my glimpses at that clock as the gropings of a spiritual eye which seeks to adjust its vision to an exact focus. The moment the focus is reached the object is epiphanised. (*SH* 189)

Here, the emphasis is not on the manifestation of a moment in the world, so much as on the quality of attention necessary to perceive that manifestation. According to his brother Stanislaus, Joyce also provided a more homely explanation of this process:

> Do you see that man who has just skipped out of the way of the tram? Consider, if he had been run over, how significant every act of his would at once become. I don't mean for the police inspector. I mean for anybody who knew him. And his thoughts, for anybody that could know them. It is my idea of the significance of trivial things that I want to give the two or three unfortunate wretches who may eventually read me.[4]

The epiphanies that Joyce worked on in the early 1900s and which grew into the stories in *Dubliners* are characterized by this same duality of the ordinary and the transfigured, as the profane or insignificant is given meaning by a certain heightening of attention, or the groping for focus that Stephen describes. On the one hand, then, the epiphany is a showing forth, a spontaneous revelation of the essence of an ordinary object: Stephen describes it in *Stephen Hero* unambiguously as the moment when 'Its soul, its whatness, leaps to us from the vesture of its appearance' (*SH* 218). On the other hand, and to the precise degree that the epiphany must be a revelation *for* some perceiving consciousness in particular, it is not essential or self-sufficient, but brought into being in, and probably also by, the act of interpretative seeing itself. On the one hand, the epiphany appears as a result of a reduction, a radical abscission of what is inessential in the object; on the other, the epiphany is achieved by an addition to the object of a certain kind of perception. On the one hand, the object is simplified; on the other, it is made more complex.

Some of the stories in *Dubliners* end with a kind of revelation, in which the reader shares the moment of enlargement of consciousness of a character. At the end of 'Araby', the young boy who has been deceived by the tawdry glamour of the bazaar suddenly feels disappointed and diminished: 'Gazing up into the darkness I saw myself as a creature driven and derided by vanity: and my eyes burned with anguish and anger' (*D*. 191). At the ending of 'A Little Cloud', the young law clerk, full of vain dreams of literary success stimulated by the vulgar bragging of his cosmopolitan friend Gallaher, makes his baby cry with a moment of roughness; the story concludes with his modest access of rueful self-knowledge: 'Little Chandler felt his cheeks suffused with shame and he stood back out of the lamplight. He listened while the paroxysm of the child's sobbing grew less and less; and tears of remorse started to his eyes' (*D*. 242).

But, in most other cases, there is no such congruence between the perceptions of character and of reader. Most of the stories end with anticlimax, incompleteness, or even concealment. 'Clay', for example, tells the story of Maria, whose quiet, contracted life is all the more poignant for the fact that she appears to be unaware of any limitation in it. Maria is subject to a cruel trick during the playing of a Hallowe'en fortune-telling game in which a person must choose one of three saucers while blindfolded; instead of the ring (betokening marriage), the prayer book (predicting the religious life), or the water (standing for emigration), the blindfolded Maria places her fingers in a saucer of clay, pointing to the inevitability of death as her only future. The story ends with Maria's incomplete singing of 'I dreamt that

I dwelt in marble halls'; instead of singing the second verse, which begins 'I dreamt that suitors sought my hand', and goes on to articulate dreams of romantic and sexual fulfilment, Maria sings the first verse all over again. Perhaps in embarrassed half-acknowledgement of the repression, her brother Joe subsides into fuddled sentimentality. The clumsy spilling of the clauses in the story's final sentence is in ironic contrast to the reticence and unconscious concealment of the story itself:

> He said that there was no time like the long ago and no music for him like poor old Balfe, whatever other people might say; and his eyes filled up so much with tears that he could not find what he was looking for and in the end he had to ask his wife to tell him where the corkscrew was. (*D*. 265)

Some of the stories actually intensify the contrast between the insight denied to the character and that asked of the reader. 'Eveline' ends with its heroine's paralysed indecision at the docks, as she is torn between boarding the ship for her new life with Frank and cleaving to her pinched, but secure, existence with her family in Dublin. The story deliberately and unequivocally blocks out any possibility of awareness on Eveline's part:

> No! No! No! It was impossible. Her hands clutched the iron in frenzy. Amid the seas she sent a cry of anguish.
>   – Eveline! Evvy!
>   He rushed beyond the barrier and called to her to follow. He was shouted at to go on, but he still called to her. She set her white face to him, passive, like a helpless animal. Her eyes gave him no sign of love or farewell or recognition. (*D*. 198)

Eveline's near-autistic retreat into non-communication and nullity is signalled not only in the flatly emphatic negations of the last phrase – 'no sign of love or farewell or recognition' - but also in the odd hiatus between the climactic sentence 'Amid the seas she sent a cry of anguish' and the crying of her name which follows it: 'Eveline! Evvy!'. The cry is in fact Frank's, as he urges her desperately to follow him; but the excision from the account of the content of Eveline's cry transfers her anguish on to Frank's words, encouraging us for a moment to misread them as her own. For a moment, we seem to hear Eveline crying her own name, in a radical dissociation from self which might be on the point of becoming reflexive self-knowledge. As we almost instantly correct the misreading, and the text lapses into the tight-lipped taciturnity of Eveline herself, the reader seems forced into an awareness of the unnegotiable gap between the momentary ascription of insight and utterance to the character and the description of the failure of insight and utterance given by the text. The epiphany here is achieved in the interval between this allowed and disavowed reflexivity.

The ending of 'A Painful Case' offers a decelerated and more self-consciously displayed version of this movement of dis-avowal and un-uttering. The fastidious, introverted scholar and writer, James Duffy, who prides himself on his austere aloofness from the pettiness of bourgeois urban life, becomes entangled in an embarrassing affair with Emily Sinico, a married woman. He breaks off the affair, and hears nothing of Emily Sinico until reading of her death after she has been hit by a railway engine while apparently inebriated. At first, Mr Duffy is revolted by the vulgarity of her end, but becomes more and more aware of his culpability:

> When he gained the crest of the Magazine Hill he halted and looked along the river towards Dublin, the lights of which burned redly and hospitably in the cold night. He looked down the slope and at the base, in the shadow of the wall of the Park, he saw some human figures lying. Those venal and furtive loves filled him with despair. He gnawed the rectitude of his life; he felt that he had been outcast from life's feast. One human being had seemed to love him and he had denied her life and happiness: he had sentenced her to ignominy, a death of shame. He knew that the prostrate creatures down by the wall were watching him and wished him gone. No one wanted him; he was outcast from life's feast. (*D.* 276)

This passage appears to be the opposite of the ending of 'Eveline'. In place of Eveline's tense inarticulacy and paralysed lack of awareness, we are given, clearly and explicitly, the stages of Mr Duffy's realization of the emptiness of his life, and the cruelty consequent upon his pose of rectitude and distance. Here, the narrative and its narration, what is said and the manner of its saying, seem to be smoothly synchronized; Joyce shows us, apparently without irony, the process whereby Duffy's life is shown to him, in all its selfish smallness. The closeness of the fit between the narrator's language and the character's – Mr Duffy is, after all, much closer in experience and character to

15

the young Joyce than any other character encountered so far in *Dubliners* – also encourages us to see this as an epiphany made available in equal measure to character and reader.

However, there is a detail of the narration which seems to prise open a chink of incongruity. 'He gnawed the rectitude of his own life; he felt that he had been outcast from life's feast', we read. The slightly self-conscious elaboration of this metaphor is forgotten as Duffy starts to articulate to himself the nature of his guilt. But this sequence ends with a repetition of the phrase, which suddenly must be read as embodying a kind of relish: 'No one wanted him; he was outcast from life's feast.' Mr Duffy, it seems, is rather pleased with this phrase. In the light of this awareness, which Mr Duffy does not share with us, the rest of his internal monologue starts to seem more like a performance than an unfolding self-confrontation. The passage is written, like much of *Dubliners*, in free indirect discourse, a third-person narration which mimics closely the lexis and idiom of the character being described. Such discourse is often employed for ironic effect in *Dubliners*, for its structure as a compromise or negotiation between the exteriority of the third person and the intimacy of the first person allows Joyce to register without openly declaring the distance between the way characters appear to themselves and how they appear to others. But the irony in this passage is more complex than this. For here we have a character who, as a writer himself, seems to employ the devices of free indirect style in his own interior monologue, and not as a means of self-exposure, but rather for self-dissimulation. Thus, we cannot be sure whether Joyce's narrative is mimicking Mr Duffy's idiom or mimicking Mr Duffy's own habit of mimicking himself. The gap between personal and literary discourse is a gap that is itself a feature of Mr Duffy's personal discourse, so that the discourse that writes about Mr Duffy in the ironically distanced third person cannot but replicate his tendency to render his own perceptions in the third person. The narrative's capacity for ironic revelation is thus itself subject to the irony that it is employed by Mr Duffy as a means of concealment. So Mr Duffy is in fact like Eveline, in moving from acknowledgement of his moral predicament to disavowal of it:

> He turned back the way he had come, the rhythm of the engine pounding in his ears. He began to doubt the reality of what memory

told him. He halted under a tree and allowed the rhythm to die away. He could not feel her near him in the darkness nor her voice touch his ear. He waited for some minutes, listening. He could hear nothing: the night was perfectly silent. He listened again: perfectly silent. He felt that he was alone. (*D*. 276–7)

As in 'Eveline', the story reaches its conclusion in negativity and denial; but here the denial is a painstakingly crafted one. We watch Mr Duffy reconstructing his invulnerability, the careful way in which Joyce composes his sentences seeming to redouble and therefore also participate in Mr Duffy's manufacture of his composure. Once again, the epiphany is virtual rather than actual, in that it is not manifested in the events or merely delivered up to the reader. It is effected, if at all, in the work of constructed understanding between character, author, and reader. Here, as elsewhere in *Dubliners*, we encounter a form of writing which is bleakly and blankly autonomous, in that it appears to efface all signs of the labour of its composition, in that 'style of scrupulous meanness' which Joyce told Grant Richards embodied his conviction 'that he is a very bold man who dares to alter in the presentment, still more to deform, whatever he has seen and heard' (*L*. ii. 134). And yet the very meanness of that writing appears highly worked, overdetermined, and dependent upon its display of the labour of artifice. Indeed, the very phrase 'scrupulous meanness' has a little ironic squirm in it. Does Joyce's 'meanness' mean to evoke the parsimony of a writing that adds nothing to what it records? Or does it point to the stinginess, mediocrity, and, indeed, unscrupulousness of the lives and sensibilities whose style he is imitating for us? Like the stories themselves, the phrase seems to give us epiphany in two different modes simultaneously: in the mode of simple, immediate revelation and the mode of self-conscious elaboration. The writing scrupulously effaces the work of writing, but continues to display the writing-labour of that effacement.

Where Joyce's later work demands attentiveness because of its excess of detail and structural intent, these stories are enigmatic because they not only withhold their meaning, but also conceal the fact of whether there *is* a hidden meaning to be distinguished. A good example of this is the story 'Two Gallants', which centres on what appears to be a plot hatched by Corley and his parasitic sidekick, Lenehan, to extract some money from a servant girl with whom Corley has taken up. The story begins with a little descriptive reverie:

> The grey warm evening of August had descended upon the city and a mild warm air, a memory of summer, circulated in the streets. The streets, shuttered for the repose of Sunday, swarmed with a gaily coloured crowd. Like illumined pearls the lamps shone from the summits of their tall poles upon the living texture below which, changing shape and hue unceasingly, sent up into the warm grey evening air an unchanging unceasing murmur. (*D*. 207)

The language here is carefully worked to evoke a dreamy glamour and poetic promise; the sentences suggest and enact the melting of distinctness – the gaily coloured crowd, the pearl-like lamps – into indistinctness: the people in the streets have become merely a 'texture', dissolving into a murmur, which then itself merges back into the 'warm grey evening air'. The slightly narcotic repetitions of the final sentence quoted bring about a circulation of verbal elements that mirrors the liquefying exchange of light and warmth evoked in the scene. This can be seen in particular in the inversion effected in the word 'unceasing': both the 'changing shape and hue' and the 'unchanging . . . murmur' of the crowd are said to be 'unceasing'. The sentence is thus balanced between excitement and ennui, its promise of novelty consumed by sameness.

The story that follows is all obliquity and dissimulation. As Corley and Lenehan arrive, Corley is at the end of a long monologue whose subject remains hidden from us. Both of the men are exploiters and parasites who live their lives according to 'shifts and intrigues' (*D*. 215); Corley exploits the affections of women, while Lenehan attaches himself to anyone who holds out the prospect of money and free drinks. It gradually becomes plain that they are discussing a stratagem involving a new girl of Corley's. The details of the plan are shrouded in secrecy and indirection. The narration attends to surfaces and appearances, coordinating Lenehan's anxiety about whether Corley will be up to the job they have in mind, and whether he will indeed share in the gains, with the reader's perplexity about what is afoot. As in 'A Painful Case', there is a parallel between the concealment, or lack of conscious acknowledgement of what is going on in the minds of the characters, and the narrative's own concealment. The story plays with the expectation of revelation, while conspiring oddly with the evasiveness or self-deceit of the characters.

Understanding is associated with various kinds of dubious illumination throughout the story; the lamps shining down upon the crowds in the first paragraph modulate into the occluded image of the moon that Lenehan anxiously inspects: 'Lenehan's gaze was fixed on the large faint moon circled with a double halo. He watched earnestly the passing of the grey web of twilight across its face' (*D.* 210). A moment later, Corley's gaze is also attracted to the moon, as he remembers one of his more notable female conquests: 'The recollection brightened his eyes. He too gazed at the pale disc of the moon, now nearly veiled' (*D.* 210); the narrative here neatly balances the brightness of Corley's desire and the obscurity of what he looks at. The figure of the moon is associated with Corley's inexpressive face, which Lenehan anxiously inspects for signs of approval, as well as with the different clocks that Lenehan consults, skipping out into the road to see the clock of Trinity College at the beginning of the evening, and noting the time by the clock of the College of Surgeons towards its end, both of them associated with Waterhouse's clock, under which Corley recalls having picked up a girl. The association with the clock of the Ballast Office in Stephen's account of the epiphany in *Stephen Hero* (see discussion above, p. 12) makes Corley's, and more particularly Lenehan's, inspection of appearances seem like a parody of what Stephen Hero describes grandly as 'the gropings of a spiritual eye which seeks to adjust its vision to an exact focus'. As he waits for Corley's return, Lenehan takes up his position, in a physically exact and symbolically appropriate way, 'in the shadow of a lamp' (*D.* 216); standing close to the base of the lamp, it is possible to benefit from its light while also remaining within the shadow cast by its shade. As with the image of the veiled moon, illumination and concealment are closely conjoined. They reappear in the memorable conclusion of the story, as Corley reveals the results of his evening to Lenehan: 'Corley halted at the first lamp and stared grimly before him. Then with a grave gesture he extended a hand towards the light and, smiling, opened it slowly to the gaze of his disciple. A small gold coin shone in the palm' (*D.* 218). What the ending of the story reveals is itself an act of revelation. But the epiphany or showing-forth of Corley's spoils is distinguished from the epiphany offered to the reader. What we see is Corley's act of display, and Lenehan's miserably covetous gaze, the religious hints in the description pointing up the ironic disparity between the two acts of showing. The description involves a complex interchange between transfiguration and materiality. What we are shown is something like the reverse of an alchemical transformation, for the gold of the coin that shines in Corley's palm is the very image of the base metal of which the two gallants are composed. And yet, in showing us the failure of transfiguration, the narrative also seems to borrow something of its discredited revelatory force. What the moment of fictional revelation shows us is that there is, after all, no mystery to reveal, that the whole intrigue has been, as we suspect, nothing but squalidly mercenary; but, in rendering this failure of transfiguration apparent, the narrative also seems to fulfil the requirement of the epiphany as described by Stephen in *Stephen Hero*: 'The soul of the commonest object, the structure of which is so adjusted, seems to us radiant. The object achieves its epiphany' (*SH* 218). The story gives us, as it were, an effulgent epitome of moral murkiness.

Throughout *Dubliners* there is a tension between these two aspects of fictional epiphany; Joyce's curious claim is that, in showing Dubliners their own paralysed soullessness, he is in fact inducing the 'soul', or essence, of Dublin. Of course, Joyce is also showing non-Dubliners this act of showing (and, in the sense that present-day Dubliners are no longer the Dubliners that Joyce was addressing, all readers of the book are now really non-Dubliners). This ambivalence is related closely to the ambivalence in the idea of the epiphany which we observed earlier; the 'soul' of Dublin's soullessness cannot be a given, a quality which can simply be manifested to the scrutinizing eye and recording pen; rather, it is a quality which must be evoked by a particular kind of transforming attention. In his 1904 postcard to Constantine Curran, we remember, Joyce used a word to describe his stories that may capture this aspect a little better than the term 'epiphany'. He called them 'epicleti', from the Greek-derived term *epiclesis*, which signifies invocation, and specifically the invocation of the presence of the Holy Ghost to consecrate the elements of the Eucharist. The stories do not manifest their meaning to the reader, but call up the reader who is necessary to construe their meaning. The genetic model of growth which governs the transition from story to story seems to propose the work of reading and understanding as a formation of such a collective reader, invoked, over and above, and even in opposition to, the more limited manifestations of understanding of the individual characters themselves. The work invokes, out of the scattered indefiniteness of vision of *Dubliners*, though without wishing to give a name or visible form to it, that collective consciousness which could be signified as 'The' *Dubliners*.

The particularity of Joyce's conception of the soul is that it involves both organic growth and conscious labour. The labour of creating the soul of Dublin is consummated in the work of the achieved work of art. Throughout *Dubliners*, Joyce implies an absolute contrast between the various kinds of work which absorb the energies of the inhabitants of Dublin, and the artistic work which both contains them and provides the model for their as yet unachieved self-understanding and self-possession – for the 'uncreated conscience of my race' which Stephen Dedalus grandly proposes to himself as the ideal of his art in *A Portrait of the Artist as a Young Man*. Throughout *Dubliners*, Joyce's attention is drawn to holidays or moments of leisure from what the narrator of 'An Encounter' calls 'the serious work of life' (*D*. 30); there is the celebratory dinner in 'After the Race', the Sunday of 'Two Gallants' and 'A Boarding House', the after-work drinking of 'A Little Cloud', 'Counterparts', and 'Ivy Day in the Committee Room', the Hallowe'en party of 'Clay', the retreat in 'Grace', and the Christmas party in 'The Dead'. This may seem to give the impression of a fluid interchange between work and life (fluidity is very much the point in 'Counterparts', for example, in which Farrington leaves the office for a quick pint in the middle of the afternoon); but, with the possible exception of 'The Dead', there is little sense that leisure offers any very meaningful alternative to work. Indeed, Joyce seems to be at pains to suggest that Dubliners are no less in thrall to monotonous and soul-destroying routines when they are at rest than when they are ostensibly at work. Thus the aimless and apparently unemployed Corley and Lenehan are in fact at work all the way through the evening, Corley working on the slavey, from whom he manages to extract the equivalent of about a month's wages, and Lenehan working on Corley in order to secure his share of the loot; Mrs Kearney is similarly anxiously negotiating her daughter's financial interests throughout the concert in 'A Mother', while Mrs Mooney devotes her Sunday to the serious work of forcing her lodger into marriage with her daughter in 'The Boarding House'.

Joyce's point would seem to be, not merely that the forms of escape or release imagined by the characters in *Dubliners* are drably inadequate or disappointing, but that they are a systematic extension of the clock-watching enclosure of the world of work. There is no more telling expression of this than the conclusion of 'Grace', which gives us, only minimally modified, the comfortable sophistries of Father Purdon, as he interprets from the pulpit a passage from St Luke's Gospel as 'a text for business men and professional men', and offers himself as the 'spiritual accountant' of the congregation (*D*. 334). All of the traditional spaces of exteriority to the world of work – the home, the pub, the concert-hall, the street, the church – turn out to be continuous and complicit with it. *Dubliners* is one of the earliest fictional intimations of the transition to that new rationalization of time pointed to by Theodor Adorno in which the rhythms and routines of capitalism come to extend themselves over every part of life; in which, in place of authentic leisure, there are merely measured quantities of 'free time'.

All the forms of work seen in *Dubliners* represent the subordination of the self rather than its enlargement and fulfilment. There are few examples in the stories of any kind of redeeming, fulfilling, or creative work. For it is only perhaps in the work of writing and reading the stories that this creative labour may be intimated. It is as though the readerly self-reflection which the stories aim to stimulate were itself to be the travail of self-making that is everywhere evaded or annulled in the stories themselves. There is, however, one exception to this account of leisure in *Dubliners*. By the time he came to write the final story, 'The Dead', Joyce had begun to reproach himself for a somewhat arrogant insensitivity to the energy and generosity of his native city:

Sometimes thinking of Ireland it seems to me that I have been unnecessarily harsh. I have reproduced (in *Dubliners* at least) none of the attractions of the city for I have never felt at ease in any city since I left it except Paris. I have not reproduced its ingenious insularity and its hospitality. (*L*. ii. 160)

In its porous openness to the public arts of song, speaking, and popular storytelling, 'The Dead' appears to bring together the public life which has been the content of many of the stories with the scrupulously aloof artfulness of their mode of telling. For almost the first time, the art of the narration is seen to converge and cooperate with its subject. The energies of observation and discrimination are here used to celebrate rather than to condemn what is written about; in the description of the food and drink, for example, which is notable not only for its abundance and quality, in contrast to the decidedly indigent levels of provision elsewhere in the collection (Maria's mislaid plum cake, Lenehan's plate of peas, Mr Duffy's unappetizing and uneaten corned beef and cabbage), but also for the opulence of the narrative attention to them. There is no other paragraph like this to be found anywhere else previously in *Dubliners*; the sumptuous enumeration of the foodstuffs anticipates the marvellous, proliferating art of the list which Joyce was to develop in his later works. At one end of the table is a goose, at the other a ham:

> Between these rival ends ran parallel lines of side dishes: two little minsters of jelly, red and yellow, a shallow dish full of blocks of blancmange and red jam, a large green leafshaped dish with a stalk-shaped handle on which lay bunches of purple raisins and peeled almonds, a companion dish on which lay a solid rectangle of Smyrna figs, a dish of custard topped with grated nutmeg, a small bowl full of chocolates and sweets wrapped in gold and silver papers and a glass vase in which stood some tall celery stalks. (*D*. 357)

Certainly, many of the same potentially stultifying influences are at work in the party as are seen in the stories that lead up to 'The Dead'; and the hold of the past over the present, in particular, seems to be a disturbing new aspect of the paralysis of Irish life. As we observed earlier, there are recollections of paralytic motifs from earlier stories – for example, in the story of Morkan's helplessly revolving horse, which recalls the stupefied, obsessive discourse of the priest in 'The Sisters' and the stranger in 'An Encounter'. We should, however, take due account of the differences between the two ends of the symbolic frame. The evocations of paralysis in the early stories of *Dubliners* are full of terror and mystery for the uncomprehending boys who come under the sinister spell of adults; the second story of paralysis is relayed to the reader in a story told for comic purposes and enlivening social effect by Gabriel Conroy, who does not, at this moment at least, appear to be conspicuously paralysed. Indeed, the celebration in 'The Dead' seems to provide an opportunity not only for Joyce to disclose a truth about Dublin life, but also for Dubliners themselves to reflect upon their life and condition. The story represents an accession of the self-consciousness that is lacking in – or denied to – the other characters. In their story-telling, the guests at the party participate in the narration in a way that is not true of the earlier stories.

It is Gabriel Conroy who is the bearer and representative of this collective consciousness. His willingness to make the speech of thanks, and, in it to accommodate his cosmopolitan progressive ideas to the traditions of Irish life, contrasts markedly with the pathological hauteur and dissociation from social responsibility of Mr Duffy, the other representative of the literary sensibility and partial self-portrait in *Dubliners*. He is not entirely comfortable with the role, of course, and is subject to criticism for his European tastes – the goloshes which he has Gretta wear, his preference for holidays in Europe rather than acquainting himself with his own country. But, by the time his speech comes to be made, the story has suggested and displayed enough of the fellowship and tolerance of the party to fill out its formulaic oratory with human significance.

What is most significant about the story, however, is the transition it makes in its final section from the outer world represented by the party to Gabriel's inner world. As the guests are getting ready to depart, Gabriel sees his wife poised on the stairs, listening to a song being sung in an upper room. Gabriel is moved by, yet also strangely detached from, the sight, which he fashions into an artistic composition:

> He asked himself what is a woman standing on the stairs in the shadow, listening to distant music, a symbol of. If he were a painter he would paint her in that attitude. Her blue felt hat would show off the bronze of her hair against the darkness and the dark panels of her skirt would show off the light ones. *Distant Music* he would call the picture if he were a painter. (D. 370)

24

At this moment, the story turns on itself to give us a kind of inverted epiphany, in which we are shown, not the image of Gretta, but Gabriel shaping her into an image. Gabriel's response to the image is appropriative and subtly self-gratifying. As the narrative follows the couple to their hotel room, Gabriel's desire for Gretta grows, heightened by reminiscence of their past. But that past is being actively and self-indulgently controlled by Gabriel's artistic consciousness.

> Like the tender fire of stars moments of their life together, that no one knew of or would ever know of, broke upon and illumined his memory. He longed to recall to her those moments, to make her forget the years of their dull existence together and remember only their moments of ecstasy. (*D*. 374)

A little like Mr Duffy, who maintains his detachment from his experience by forming sentences about it, the intensity of the past is embodied for Gabriel in the memory of his own words about it, written in a letter to Gretta: 'In one letter he had written to her then he had said: *Why is it that words like these seem to me so dull and cold? Is it because there is no word tender enough to be your name?*' (*D*. 374). The reappearance, a little later in Gabriel's implied interior monologue, of the phrase 'distant music', the title that he has given his imaginary portrait of Gretta a little earlier in the evening alerts us to the self-indulgence involved here. Earlier on, the title had evoked concealment and mystery; the painting that Gabriel imagines must point beyond itself to the music that paint cannot represent. But at the same time, the title of the painting, by its very act of designation, captures the music that it suggests is beyond the power of the image to enclose. Now, the return of the title indicates Gabriel's attempt to bring together past and future, composing the scene of his imminent seduction of Gretta just as he refashions their past:

> Like distant music those words that he had written years before were borne towards him from the past. He longed to be alone with her. When the others had gone away, when he and she were in the room of their hotel, then they would be alone together. He would call her softly:
> – Gretta!
> Perhaps she would not hear at once: she would be undressing. Then something in his voice would strike her. She would turn and look at him . . . (*D*. 375)

25

In delicately indicting Gabriel's in itself hardly culpable self-indulgence, the story seems to be separating itself from its own epiphanic mode, its own tendency to subject disparate lives and experiences to the condensing and simplifying work of writing. When Gabriel asks his wife about the music to which she has been listening, he will discover that it has summoned up not memories of their own life together, but the memory of Michael Furey, a young boy from Galway who had loved Gretta and died. This brings about suddenly a

> shameful consciousness of his own person . . . [as] a ludicrous figure, acting as a pennyboy for his aunts, a nervous well-meaning senti-mentalist, orating to vulgarians and idealising his own clownish lusts, the pitiable fatuous fellow he had caught a glimpse of in the mirror. (D. 380)

Although this is sometimes seen as the moment of Gabriel's insight into himself, there is in fact the same discrepancy as in other stories in the collection between the knowledge given to a character and that indicated to the reader – for Gabriel is still freezing his feelings and judgements into the form of an image, albeit the mirror-image of himself rather than the painterly image of Gretta. The narration reveals the limits of revelation, epipha-nizes the danger of epiphanic thinking. In fact, Gabriel will attain a position of representative consciousness in and for the book, not by appropriation, not by an act of wilful self-constitution, but in the final moments in which he turns to and embraces what cannot be gathered into the self, cannot be rendered as a work. The famous passage which concludes 'The Dead' by evoking the falling of the snow all over Ireland is diffusive and excessive, where so much of the writing of the book had worked to concentrate and limit.

> Yes, the newspapers were right: snow was general all over Ireland. It was falling on every part of the dark central plain, on the treeless hills, falling softly upon the Bog of Allen and, farther westward, softly falling into the dark mutinous Shannon waves. It was falling, too, upon every part of the lonely churchyard on the hill where Michael Furey lay buried. It lay thickly drifted on the crooked crosses and headstones, on the spears of the little gates, on the barren thorns. His soul swooned softly as he heard the snow falling faintly through the universe and faintly falling, like the descent of their last end, upon all the living and the dead. (D. 384)

The words and cadences call attention to themselves, in their alliterations and repetitions, but they also point beyond themselves. The snow is the principle of reconciliation and unity, between passionate youth and temperate age, the past and the present, Ireland and Europe. But it is also the principle of generality ('snow was general all over Ireland'), a dissolving, edgeless, generative drift. The passage describes and enacts relinquishment rather than mastery, and Gabriel becomes himself at the moment at which he loses himself. Similarly, the book becomes itself in the moment of losing its bearings. The consummation of the work, which everything leads us to expect to see coinciding with the advent of fulfilled self-knowledge in the interpreting self, is achieved, not in a working out, but a working loose of these tight equivalences. The interest of *Dubliners* lies, not in its evolution from the incoherence of snapshots or impressions into the wholeness of a completed work, but in the manner in which it continues to work against its own desire for definition and self-completion. Strangely, perhaps, it is this that will confirm its continuity with the rest of Joyce's work.

3

Workshop and Labyrinth: *A Portrait of the Artist as a Young Man*

By 1906, as he was writing the later stories in what was to become *Dubliners*, Joyce had written 1,000 or so manuscript pages of an autobiographical novel, to which he gave the title *Stephen Hero*. This novel appears to have been designed to actualize, at length and in abundance, the affirmation of soul or self that Joyce had declared to be inhibited or absent in Dublin life. It was a fiction-alized autobiography, which followed through the formation of the artistic personality of Stephen Dedalus, in reaction against the narrowing and constraining influences of family, church, and state. Where *Dubliners* was caught between the desire to portray the soullessness of Irish life, and the compulsion to evoke that soul through its writing, *Stephen Hero* offers a much more emphatic and visible display of what Keats called 'soul-making'.[1] The self whose formation Joyce set out to affirm and display in *Stephen Hero* was no longer an implicit, collective self, but a real-ized, individual self. The pages of the novel that survive cover Stephen's years at University College Dublin, years in which he is forming his artistic consciousness and conscience. The narra-tive is for the most part a series of reports on encounters between the isolated, sensitive, and stubborn young aesthete and the narrowness, conformity, and squalor of the world that surrounds him. In nearly all of these encounters, Stephen is shown as victo-rious, either through the exercise of devastating polemic, or by maintaining a haughty silence which lures his adversaries into betraying their vulgarity and narrowness. Many of Stephen's encounters with other characters are in the form of exchanges designed to exemplify Stephen's superiority of intellect and spirit. We are given fragments of conversations with the fellow-student McCann, a feminist and advanced thinker, which purport to show Stephen riddling his theories 'with agile bullets' (*SH* 49); we are supposed similarly to enjoy Stephen's outwitting of the muscular nationalist Madden, who argues for the ennobling and purifying influence of Gaelic sports (*SH* 60–3); and to approve of Stephen's dogged discomfiture of Father Dillon, the President of the College, who wishes to prohibit the delivery of his paper on aesthetics (*SH* 84–91), as well as the rather more economical way in which he disposes of Father Artifoni's objections to an allusion to Bruno:

> – You know, he said, the writer, Bruno, was a terrible heretic.
> – Yes, said Stephen, and he was terribly burned.
>
> (*SH* 153)

Where *Dubliners* had been written with a 'scrupulous meanness' of style, *Stephen Hero* is characterized by a spendthrift explicitness about the grounds of Stephen's disaffection from his family, church, and country. We are told repeatedly about Stephen's labour to create himself as an artist: 'He persuaded himself that it is necessary for an artist to labour incessantly at his art if he wishes to express completely even the simplest conception' (*SH* 34). But the narrative gives us no sense of the process of this labour – for Stephen seems already to have achieved a full and authoritative comprehension of his nature. The narrative is the remorselessly idealizing mirror in which Stephen's egotism, rage, and resentment are translated into noble artistic purpose. It affects to show us Stephen's struggle to escape from repression and hypocrisy; but the qualities of absolute command and explicitness displayed in the narrative cancel out all dubiety and conflict. The narrative, we might say, is the factitiously perfected self-consciousness of the character. One particularly disturbing example of this is the account of the funeral of Stephen's sister Isabel, which leads Stephen to the following disagreeable reflections:

> The entire apparatus of the State seemed to him at fault from its first to its last operation. No young man can contemplate the fact of death with extreme satisfaction and no young man, specialized by fate or her step-sister chance for an organ of sensitiveness and intellectiveness, can contemplate the network of falsities and trivialities which

make up the funeral of a dead burgher without extreme disgust. (*SH* 151–2)

Typically, we are given no details of the 'falsities and trivialities' which are said to lead so inevitably to Stephen's high-minded disdain. The contrivance of the second sentence, with its structure of doubling ('No young man ... and no young man') and thickening subordinate clauses, is intended to manifest the very qualities of 'sensitiveness and intellectiveness' of which it speaks; but the sentence succeeds only in interposing the ungainly bulk of Stephen's self-dramatization between the reader and its object. The consciousness which has wrought these phrases – or rather, perhaps, the consciousness which these phrases bring into being as their putative originator – displays itself as the very opposite of an 'organ of sensitiveness and intellectiveness' – as an organ of dullness and imposture. What renders this passage and the book it exemplifies so deeply unsatisfactory is the absence of cues which would sanction the possibility that this is an ironic imposture of Stephen's posturing.

The extravagant explicitness of *Stephen Hero* is achieved via strict disavowal. It became possible for Joyce to write the emergence of Stephen's soul only at the cost of denying everything in Stephen's world which is believed to constrain or oppose that emergence. The selfhood that is formed in *Stephen Hero* depends in fact upon processes of extrication from and transcendence of the everyday, in a confirmation of the model of male selfhood that has been described by Nancy Chodorow and other feminist psychoanalysts.[2] In this model, the male infant, which originally experiences oneness with the body of the mother, from which it must gradually separate, comes to conceive of its own identity (and, later on, of identity as such) in terms of splitting, separation, and aggressive denial of the female. Thus the social world, and the 'world' itself, in so far as they are experienced as impediments to the realization of self, are conceived of as both maternal and material, the maternal having been reduced to the condition of pure, nescient materiality.

There is an episode at the end of chapter XXII of the novel which brings this aspect of Stephen's attitude to the fore. Here, Stephen's mother disturbs his melancholy piano-playing with a panicky report of a crisis in his sister's illness:

He desisted from his chords and waited, bending upon the keyboard in silence: and his soul commingled itself with the assailing, inarticulate dusk. A form which he knew for his mother's appeared far down in the room, standing in the doorway. In the gloom, her excited face was crimson. A voice which he remembered as his mother's, a voice of a terrified human being, called his name. The form at the piano answered:
    – Yes?
    – Do you know anything about the body?

(SH 147)

Stephen is tangled in ambivalence here. He is seeking to sink back into passive oneness, or 'commingling', with the 'assailing, inarticulate' dusk of the world of nescient forms which he finds both threatening and deeply alluring, though the coupling of threat and inarticulateness leaves it unclear whether the dusk is assailing *and* inarticulate, or assailing *because* it is inarticulate. Almost straightaway, his mother appears, like the personification of this pure, impersonal materiality. But if Stephen's mother is identified with the 'assailing, inarticulate dusk', she also brings about an unwelcome disturbance of the luxurious reverie into which Stephen has sunk; inarticulately, she assails Stephen's dream of commingling with the 'assailing, inarticulate dusk'. The groping, desperate exchange that follows appears to be intended to illustrate Stephen's mother's pathetic inability to speak of the body, even at a time of illness and death; for her, the body, and especially the female body, becomes a terrifying and unrepresentable 'hole':

    – What ought I do? There's some matter coming away from the hole in Isabel's... stomach... Did you ever hear of that happening?
    – I don't know, he answered trying to make sense of her words, trying to say them again to himself.
    – Ought I send for the doctor... Did you ever hear of that?...
What ought I do?
    – I don't know? What hole?
    – The hole... the hole we all have... here.

(SH 147)

In trying to articulate the process of bodily evacuation and dissolution ('matter coming away from the hole in Isabel's... stomach'), Stephen's mother's own words are hollowed by ellipsis and evasion. She cannot speak of the body, perhaps, because she is identified so closely with it. Later on, in the opening chapter of *Ulysses*, Stephen's mother is again to be associated with the horrors of bodily dissolution, or the horror of the maternal body *as* a dissolution, in Stephen's memory of the 'bowl of white china [which] stood beside her bedstead holding the green sluggish bile which she had torn up from her rotting liver by fits of loud groaning vomiting' (*U.* 5. 1. 108–10) (Stephen's mother's illness is not identified in *Ulysses*, but Joyce's own mother died of liver cancer). In this passage from *Stephen Hero*, Stephen's mother is thus at once collapsed into the condition of a pure body-consciousness and accused of a crippling dissociation from the body.

But, in this passage from *Stephen Hero*, Stephen, and the narrative that speaks in his name, is afflicted by the same simultaneous engulfment and dissociation that paralyses his mother's speech. For Stephen, the mother's inarticulate terror appears as unrepresentable as the body that she herself finds so terrifyingly unspeakable. This is a rare moment in *Stephen Hero*, because it shows Stephen detached from, and struggling to regain, his narrative authority and detachment. Attempting both to integrate his mother into his aesthetic reverie of form and colour and to hold her helpless terror at a distance, Stephen can make no sense of her words, not even by saying them over again to himself. The unrepresentability of his mother is exactly equivalent to the unrepresentability of the body for his mother. We thus cannot be sure whether this moment in *Stephen Hero* is the representation of a gap in consciousness and language, or *is that gap itself*; whether the narrative detaches Stephen from the scene, or envelops him in its troubling vacuity.

The problem that Joyce seems to have encountered through the writing of *Stephen Hero* was that the fulfilment of heroic selfhood can be displayed only by a neurotic denial of the embeddedness and embodiedness that is necessary to it. The circumstances of Stephen's life are there merely in order for Stephen to be shown striving and prevailing against them. Even in the pages of the novel that survive, Stephen's remorseless intellectual and rhetorical victories over the enemies to his freedom become hugely wearisome. The pages of the novel seem so laborious precisely because there is no imaginative work left to be done. Stephen's artistic being is said to be the fruit of long spiritual travail, but has in fact always already been achieved. Thus, if in one sense the artistic character of Stephen is the result of a heroic refusal of *petit bourgeois* sensibility and religious dogma, in another sense he remains perfectly negative, no more than a slim precipitate of the will to negation. Stephen's substance, along with that of the book that speaks so obstinately on his behalf, comes to be consumed by the intensity of its desire to resist assimilation.

In one sense the narrative style of *Stephen Hero* is a flagrant contradiction of the aesthetic that Stephen himself begins to articulate in it, and which is carried over, in significantly extended form, into *A Portrait of the Artist as a Young Man*. In *Stephen Hero*, Stephen decides that all art is divided into three types: the lyrical, in which 'the artist sets forth his image in immediate relation to himself', the epical, in which 'the artist sets forth his image in immediate relation to himself and to others', and the dramatic, in which 'the artist sets forth his image in immediate relations to others' (*SH* 72). By the time of *A Portrait of the Artist as a Young Man*, the neutral division of types has become an evolutionary progression, in which dramatic art, now more fully and clearly defined as that art in which 'the vitality which has flowed and eddied round each person fills every person with such vital force that he or she assumes a proper and intangible aesthetic life' (*P*. 215), is presented as the highest form of art. One of the most obvious reasons for Joyce's dissatisfaction with *Stephen Hero* is that he had already, in many of the stories in *Dubliners*, developed a way of absenting himself as author, in order to give the impression that the characters being written about are, in a sense, the agents of the writing, in that the language of the narrative borrows or mimics what we may feel to be their characteristic idioms. Examples of this principle at work in *Dubliners* might include the childish, repetitive language of 'Clay', which appears to mimic the style of thought and speech of Maria, and the beginning of 'The Dead', which famously borrows the maidservant's grammatical solecism: 'Lily, the caretaker's daughter, had been literally run off her feet . . .' (*D*. 336). Hugh Kenner names this feature of Joyce's writing the 'Uncle Charles Principle', after a character introduced early in *A Portrait of the Artist as a Young Man* whose characteristic idioms Joyce allows momentarily to

33

appropriate the narrative language of his book. The important word in the phrase 'Every morning, therefore, Uncle Charles repaired to his outhouse' (*P*. 81) is that stiffly novelistic 'repaired', which, Kenner tells us, 'would be Uncle Charles's own word should he choose to say what he is doing'.[3] In *Ulysses*, we will see this principle extended so that the narrative is taken over and spoken through not just by characters, but also by physical moods, conditions, and situations; it is as if Joyce were concerned to find more and more opportunities for the work itself, as it were, to extrude its own consciousness, memory, and idiom, in a process that we might call 'mimetic autonomism'. Mimetic autonomism reproduces and elaborates the ironies attaching to narrative epiphany in *Dubliners*. In that it allows the referential subject or context of the writing to speak for itself, it appears to give that subject autonomy from the muddling and muffling purposes of the author. But this very emancipation may also mean that the writing itself begins to exercise and extend its own workings, autonomous both of authorial direction and of referential grounding. Once liberated, the work of mimesis begins to mimic itself, and its own workings.

When contrasted with this movement in Joyce's writing, *Stephen Hero* seems like an aberration indeed. Where the rest of his work looks for ways to evade or suppress the governing authorial perspective and the spurious 'objectivity' with which it was identified, the narration of *Stephen Hero* exercises a lumbering tyranny over the reader. Joyce forces his will upon the book, using the central character of Stephen, along with the characters with whom he comes into contact, as the merest kind of instrument for his own self-enlargement, and arrogantly attributing to Stephen the rhetorical and intellectual power that he himself desired so ardently. In appearing to describe the process of self-making in Stephen, Joyce is actively carrying through that process on his own behalf, in a massive act of self-justification. The deadening hold which the third-person narrative has over the reader, enforcing continuously the view of Stephen as Promethean outsider and announcing its heroizing intention in every detail of the text, soon becomes as intolerable for the reader as it did for Joyce himself.

But, at the same time, and by a curious logic of intensification, there is also a sense in which *Stephen Hero* begins to resemble the fictional procedures of *Dubliners* and *Ulysses*. So forced and fixated is Stephen's posture of heroic refusal that it begins to harden into a kind of mask, or carapace. It is as though the work had begun to generate its own style, which, borrowing from Joyce's later descriptions of the styles of *Ulysses*, we might designate 'aesthetic gigantism'. There is a moment at the beginning of chapter XX which seems to crystallize this movement. After his successful interview with the President of the College, Stephen enjoys the admiration of his fellows, as well as of his brother:

> Maurice listened to his brother's account of his battle with recognized authority, but he made no remark upon it. Stephen himself, in default of another's service, began to annotate the incident copiously, expanding every suggestive phase of the interview. He consumed much imaginative fuel in this diverting chase of the presumable. (*SH* 92)

There is only the smallest tremor of irony in this account of Stephen having to become his own narrator; for it points to the curious growth in the degree of Stephen's command, not only over his own language, but over the language of the book. The morose, elaborate self-display of the narrative comes to seem more and more like the mimetic precipitate of Stephen's character, rather than, or as well as, the reliable testimony of a too-partisan author. In growing into its 'own' language, in confirmation of the principle of mimetic autonomism identified a little earlier, the book also grows apart from itself; at such moments, the book's extravagant self-display can begin to be read as an ironic impersonation of the kind of book that Stephen might be likely to write at this point, though it is an impersonation without ethical purpose and intent, an irony without orientation. Another example occurs when we read of Stephen's disappointment in his friend Madden, to whom he has given his paper on aesthetics to read: 'When a demand for intelligent sympathy goes unanswered he is too stern a disciplinarian who blames himself for having offered a dullard an opportunity to participate in the warmer movement of a more highly organized life' (*SH* 78). I honestly do not know whether or not to recommend that the reader laugh at this sentence. Again, it is hard to know whether to take this as a particularly egregious example of Joyce's determination to defend and exalt his fictional *alter ego* against every reverse, or as an elaborate mimicry of the elaborate (and specious) self-vindication that we have come to see as typical of Stephen. Joyce might in fact already at this moment have written the wry sentence in 'A Painful Case' which describes Mr Duffy's similar propensity to self-narration: 'He had an odd autobiographical habit which led him to compose in his mind from time to time a short sentence about himself containing a subject in the third person and a predicate in the past tense' (*D*. 267). I am not here trying to suggest, against my earlier judgement about the absence of redeeming irony in the book, any sustained ironic intention in Joyce's presentation of the Stephen of *Stephen Hero*, only to suggest that, in its approving duplication of Stephen's egotistic self-absorption, the narrative cannot help becoming at times an imitation or acting-out of Stephen's own performance of himself. The more Joyce sought to subdue his autobiographical novel to his own aesthetic programme, and the more he strove to maintain the alliance between himself and his character, the more his novel threatened to grow its own life, separate from him. Late in his life, Joyce dismissed the novel as 'a schoolboy's production';[4] this conventional phrase may have a more exact truth than the writer intended, for it points to the manner in which the schoolboy's consciousness was already governing the novel in spite of the author's intentions.

When Joyce abandoned this novel in 1907 or 1908, and set to writing *A Portrait of the Artist as a Young Man*, he abandoned the authoritative third-person narration of *Stephen Hero*, in an attempt to find a way of presenting Stephen's thoughts and feelings more immediately. This is Joyce's version of the struggle, in which many modernist writers were engaged, to find an art of direct showing rather than an art of oblique telling. In making this choice, Joyce was not only breaking off from the mode of narration of *Stephen Hero*; he was also accelerating and intensifying the tendency within it to mimetic autonomization. Allowing the perceptions and language of the central character to become dominant in *A Portrait of the Artist as a Young Man* was designed, not only to enlarge this tendency in *Stephen Hero*, but also to control it. Curiously, then, we can see the abandonment of the embarrassingly over-explicit narrative control of *Stephen Hero*, not so much as a surrender to what Stephen identifies as the 'dramatic' form of art, which lets the story tell itself in its own idiom, as an attempt to exercise a greater control over its workings and implications. In *A Portrait of the Artist as a Young Man*, Joyce developed the consequences of a work that was not simply the product or expression of a pre-existing artistic intention, but the result of a generative process that originated in and was prolonged in the work itself. *A Portrait of the Artist as a Young Man* is the first of Joyce's works to work on itself in this systematic way.

In *A Portrait of the Artist as a Young Man*, Stephen accepted the dissociation of artist and subject which he had resisted in *Stephen Hero*. Relieved of the burden of speaking for Stephen, and able to accept him as a character, rather than as a magnified and idealized version of himself, Joyce was able to render his thoughts, experiences, and impulses with more force and intimacy than had previously been possible. Following the lead of Henry James and Joseph Conrad, Joyce bartered breadth for intensity. *A Portrait of the Artist as a Young Man* gives us little of the realistic environment, social or physical, that is supplied in *Stephen Hero*. Here, we must make sense of Stephen's experiences, as he does, from the inside out, and without external guidance. Joyce holds to the principle of restricted point of view much more consistently in this novel than any writer hitherto, especially in the early sections of the novel dealing with Stephen's childhood, which discover a particular richness in the very simplicity and poverty of childish perceptions. There is no better example of this than the description of Stephen's beating by the prefect of studies at Clongowes. Joyce brilliantly reproduces the effect of sensory saturation as Stephen is struck:

> Stephen closed his eyes and held out in the air his trembling hand with the palm upwards. He felt the prefect of studies touch it for a moment at the fingers to straighten it and then the swish of the sleeve of the soutane as the pandybat was lifted to strike. A hot burning stinging tingling blow like the loud crack of a broken stick made his trembling hand crumple together like a leaf in the fire: and at the sound and the pain scalding tears were driven into his eyes. His whole body was shaking with fright, his arm was shaking and his crumpled burning livid hand shook like a loose leaf in the air. A cry sprang to his lips, a prayer to be let off. But though the tears scalded his eyes and his limbs quivered with pain and fright he held back the hot tears and the cry that scalded his throat. (P. 71)

The narrative here fails to keep pace with the sudden rush of sensation. The words tumble out in panicky approximation, the senses of touch and sound driven together: 'a hot burning sting-ing tingling blow like the loud crack of a broken stick'. The paragraph is written in formal sentences, though they are agi-tated to the point of bursting by the overload of mingled feeling that they attempt to convey and contain. The effect of immediacy is brought about by the very incapacity of the language to keep up with Stephen's feelings: it is important that the passage records, not just the succession of those feelings, but the effect of their unrepresentable intensity. In its temporary surrender of control and proportion, the language corresponds to Stephen's loss of command and sense of self at the moment of the assault; but by the time the reader has recognized this correspondence, the language has already re-established some measure of self-conscious control over the experience. So the individual sentences in the paragraph and the paragraph as a whole construct a dou-ble temporality; they oscillate between the sense of a language driven asunder by the unrepresentable intensity of what they represent and the sense of a language carefully simulating the effect of this near-disintegration. The reader is both vividly and claustrophobically inside the experience and ecstatically to one side of it. The passage displays the falling-short of mimesis in the very intensity of its mimetic success, the final complexity being that this is *part of* its mimetic effect; for, if the reader is both inside and outside the experience, then this reproduces the manner in which Stephen himself is at once helplessly passive and defen-sively distanced from himself during the beating. As with the episode from *Stephen Hero* discussed earlier in this chapter (see above, pp. 30-2), it is hard to decide whether this is a dissociated rendering of an intense experience, or an intensely mimetic ren-dering of an experience of dissociation. To borrow again the terms suggested by the mature Stephen later in the book, the passage seems at once to be lyrical and dramatic. It is lyrical in that it is 'the simplest verbal vesture of an instant of emotion', and in that 'he who utters it is more conscious of the instant of emotion than of himself as feeling emotion' (*P.* 214). But it is also dramatic, in that it is not only the simple expression, but also the reconstruc-tion and display of unselfconscious feeling; in it, 'the personality of the artist. . . impersonalizes itself' (ibid.), in order not to displace or distort its moment of intense feeling.

The passage is an example of the most important stylistic principle that Joyce discovered and developed in *A Portrait of the Artist as a Young Man* – namely, the interiorization of artistic command. Where *Stephen Hero* suggests at every point the existence of an authorial viewpoint separate from and in excess of what is being narrated, *A Portrait of the Artist as a Young Man* allows itself no such reliably exteriorized interpretative perspective. Although Joyce was neither alone in discovering, nor the first to reap the rewards of, a restriction of point of view in narrative, *A Portrait of the Artist as a Young Man* combines this technique with another extraordinary innovation – namely, the rendering of a growing consciousness with a style or succession of styles that themselves appear to develop and grow.

Thus, the childish impressions that are gathered at the beginning of the novel are rendered in a language which approximates closely to the level of linguistic development we can assume in Stephen at that age. There are no complex or subordinated grammatical structures, and the narrative consists for the most part of simple statements pinned down by indicative verbs, and linked by the elementary propositions 'and' and 'but'; it is some way into the narrative that we encounter the first 'because', presumably because the attribution of cause comes later in the child's development than the recognition of simple association. The structure of the sentences appears to follow closely the structure of Stephen's thought, for both are organized around patterns of antithesis, of colours, smells, and sensations: 'There were two cocks that you turned and water came out: cold and hot. He felt cold and then a little hot: and he could see the names printed on the cocks' (*P*. 30). It seems appropriate indeed that Stephen is in 'the class of elements' at Clongowes Wood College; at this stage, his view of the world and the language which renders it are indeed elementary, in being focused around clearly separable items of perception, which can as yet be combined only in very primitive ways. Of course, Joyce is establishing his relationship between the style and content of Stephen's perceptions by means of a rather fragile circularity. We do not first encounter Stephen's impressions and then verify the appropriateness of the language in which they are rendered. Rather it is the language itself which suggests the undeveloped or elementary consciousness of Stephen, which we then, as though subsequently to our recognition of this consciousness, seem to see reinforced by the 'appropriate' language in which it is rendered.

The most signal advantage of this method of telling a story is that it deals with the problem of the incongruence of ends and beginnings. Other autobiographical novels and *Bildungsromans* (or novels of growth and development) had always had to find other ways of concealing the superior knowledge of the author, and subduing the acquired authority of first-person authorial language. Dickens's method at the beginning of *Great Expectations*, on which *A Portrait of the Artist as a Young Man* may actually draw to some degree, is to keep the reader's attention focused narrowly on the thoughts and feelings of the young Pip, though he cannot entirely suppress the signs of an organizing, alien authorial presence. The disadvantage for Dickens of rendering childish feeling in the language of the adult narrator is that he is compelled to place the events of his narrative in a stable and specified temporal frame. The conscientious avoidance or unavailability of the language of time at the beginning of *A Portrait of the Artist as a Young Man* prevents the imposition of the authority of retrospection:

> Once upon a time and a very good time it was there was a
> moocow coming down along the road and this moocow that was
> coming down along the road met a nicens little boy named baby
> tuckoo . . .
>
> His father told him that story: his father looked at him through
> a glass: he had a hairy face.
>
> He was baby tuckoo. The moocow came down the road where
> Betty Byrne lived: she sold lemon platt.
>
> > *O, the wild rose blossoms*
> > *On the little green place.*
>
> He sang that song. That was his song.
>
> > *O, the geen wothe botheth.*
>
> (*P*. 25)

To begin a novel with the immemorial 'once upon a time' of fairy-tale is a nicely judged tease. If we compare this beginning in imagination with the ways in which it might have been rendered in the language of a more conventional novel of childhood or autobiographical reminiscence, it will soon become clear how little temporal and spatial placement we are permitted in Joyce's novel. For what we are emphatically *not* given is a sentence like this: 'Stephen always looked forward to the stories told to him before bedtime by his father, an ironic, hirsute man, who winked at him confidentially through his whisky glass as he spoke'; or like this: 'In later years, Stephen Dedalus, author and renegade, was never to forget his first encounter with the art of fiction . . .'. The fragments which form this achronological overture to *A Portrait of the Artist as a Young Man* are not so much timeless as temporally overimplicated. Here it is uncertain whether we are being presented an accelerated narrative sequence making up one episode in that childhood, or a series of moments of awareness given in the order in which they are deposited in Stephen's memories, or an ensemble of memories put together at some later point in Stephen's development. We cannot be certain of the order, the duration, or the frequency of any of the elements in the opening pages, or, indeed, whether they are meant to form any sequence at all. The fragments can neither be digested within, nor clearly held apart from the temporal sequence that develops in the novel.

It appears that we enter the conventionally successive time of narrative with the description of the football game at Clongowes Wood College. Now we have distinctions of tense that seem to place the narrative at a particular vantage point in time: 'The wide playgrounds were swarming with boys. . . . He kept on the fringe of his line. . . . Rody Kickham was a decent fellow but Nasty Roche was a stink. . . . And one day he had asked: – What is your name?' (*P*. 26–7). The second section of the novel's first chapter seems to extend over about twenty-four hours, from the afternoon of the football game, to the following afternoon, which finds Stephen ill in the school infirmary. The discriminations of the language both give the reader temporal placing and convey the sense that Stephen is not capable of defining his experience. However, there is not exact or literal correspondence between the rate of Stephen's growth and the rate at which the language of the narrative develops. Although only twenty-four hours seem to have passed between the beginning and the end of the second section of the novel, its climactic evocation of the death of Parnell, with whom Stephen associates himself in his luxuriously

41

melancholic fantasy, seems already to emanate from a much more sophisticated literary consciousness:

> He saw the sea of waves, long dark waves rising and falling, dark under the moonless night. A tiny light twinkled at the pierhead where the ship was entering: and he saw a multitude of people gathered by the waters' edge to see the ship that was entering their harbour. . . . And he saw Dante in a maroon velvet dress and with a green velvet mantle hanging from her shoulders walking proudly and silently past the people who knelt by the waters' edge. (P. 46–7)

As Stephen grows, the language of the book grows more complex and versatile; or perhaps we should say that the growing complexity and versatility of the language suggest equivalent growth of awareness in Stephen. Sentences grow longer, vocabulary enlarges, subordinated grows out of coordinated syntax, adverbs and adjectives thicken and discriminate the sense, and metaphors are more self-consciously deployed and sustained. At times, the narrative almost seems to flaunt its acquisition of certain stylistic accomplishments, as in the playful relish in relative clauses displayed in the following passage describing Stephen's walks with his father and grand-uncle:

> Trudging along the road or standing in some grimy wayside public house, his elders spoke constantly of the subjects nearer their hearts, of Irish politics, of Munster and of the legends of their own family, to all *of which* Stephen lent an avid ear. Words *which* he did not understand he said over and over to himself till he had learnt them by heart . . . in secret he began to make ready for the great part *which* he felt awaited him the nature *of which* he only dimly apprehended. (P. 83; emphasis added)

One of the most impressive discoveries of *A Portrait of the Artist as a Young Man* is that growth into one's own distinctive language is in fact a process of adjustment to the language of others, as it is encountered through reading, instruction, and the discourses of social life. If the book shows Stephen striving towards an ideal of linguistic self-possession, it also shows in its very narrative form that such self-possession can arise only out of a condition in which one is possessed or spoken through by the language of others. It is for this reason perhaps that, at crucial stages of the narrative, Joyce appears to suspend his own principle of restricted point of view, by having Stephen's receiving and responding consciousness recede from the narrative. During the account of the political argument over Christmas dinner, and in the evocation of the torments of Hell by Father Arnall during the retreat at Clongowes, Stephen is present in the novel only as an abstract receptivity, as a kind of diaphragm vibrating to the force of what he hears. The horrified emptying-out and invasion of Stephen's awareness by what he later characterizes as 'the din of all the hollowsounding voices' (*P.* 106) is the whole point.[5]

As the novel proceeds, and Stephen becomes aware of and begins to resist the work of language upon him, the question of narrative authority becomes more and pressing. Stephen's emerging political awareness of the linguistic subordination of Ireland is congruent with the more general vulnerability of the self to alien voices, and its permeation by them, that is apparent throughout the book. During a conversation with the Dean of Studies at University College, who is an English convert to Catholicism, Stephen reflects:

> The language in which we are speaking is his before it is mine. How different are the words *home*, *Christ*, *ale*, *master*, on his lips and on mine! I cannot speak or write these words without unrest of spirit. His language, so familiar and so foreign, will always be for me an acquired speech. I have not made or accepted its words. My voice holds them at bay. My soul frets in the shadow of his language. (*P.* 216)

This passage gives an explicitly cultural–political dimension to the spiritual–aesthetic concerns of Joyce's early writing. The preoccupation with the work of soul-making, which has come gradually to be identified with the forging of an authentic language for the self, is here seen against the background of a colonial history in which, as it is at this moment perceived by Stephen, the self's dissociation from itself derives from a peculiarly Irish sense of alienation from the language of the oppressor. Where other Irish writers turned away from English, or attempted to Gaelicize it, Joyce, like Beckett after him, will slowly abandon the dream of an authentic language of the self, and explore instead the implications of a condition in which all language is both 'familiar and foreign', both self-made and 'acquired speech'. Joyce will slowly forge a language which is

Irish precisely in its lack of autogenetic authenticity, and in its reverse colonization of the colonizing language of English.

As *A Portrait of the Artist as a Young Man* progresses, its language seems designed to match and embody Stephen's steadily enlarging self-confidence and critical awareness, accompanied as these necessarily seem to be by a corresponding narrowing of responsiveness and receptivity. By the later stages of the book, the gap of competence between the narrative and Stephen's interior monologue seems to have thinned to almost nothing. Narrative and monologue mirror each other, since the narration of Stephen's interior monologue necessarily seems to mimic the habit of self-narrativization that characterizes that monologue, or, putting it the other way round, the way in which the monologue attempts to anticipate the narrative form in which it will be rendered:

> The images he had summoned gave him no pleasure. They were secret and inflaming, but her image was not entangled by them. That was not the way to think of her. It was not even the way in which he thought of her. Could his mind then not trust itself? (P. 261–2)

In fact, this collapse of the distinction between narration and narrated is signalled in the literal replacement of third-person narrative by first-person narrative in the sequence of journal entries that end the book. The narrative authority that in *Stephen Hero* had been assumed in advance and crudely enlisted on behalf of Stephen is here shown to be the long and laborious achievement of the book and its central character.

Conventionally, the *Bildungsroman* charts a move from irresponsibility to responsibility, from the private to the social self, from dissociation to integration. In the modernist *Bildungsroman* – of which *A Portrait of the Artist as a Young Man* is, of course, a notable example – the protagonist tends to have achieved, or to be left on the point of achieving, integration with himself or herself, rather than integration of the self with society. *A Portrait of the Artist as a Young Man* accords with this pattern, but also gives it a distinctively Joycian wrench. For the achievement of Stephen's integrated selfhood involves his move into the position of author of his own life. It is not, as some critics have wanted to suggest, that Stephen is literally offered as the author of the book we have been reading; it is rather that, by the end of the novel, he comes to see his own life as possessing, or potentially disclosing, the same qualities of intelligibility and integration as the literary work that has rendered it.

This process has been prepared for by the thickening of introspection and reflexivity in the last third of the book. As it focuses Stephen's memories of his own earlier life, the book begins, as it were, to re-read itself in the manner in which Stephen urgently, even obsessively, reads himself. The most important and conspicuous manner in which this is brought about is through Stephen's growing consciousness of the mythical pattern buried in his own name. In Greek mythology, Daedalus was a scientist and inventor who was responsible, among other things, for fashioning the labyrinth upon the island of Crete in which was confined the man-eating Minotaur. After incurring the displeasure of Minos, the king of Crete, Daedalus and his son Icarus were confined in the labyrinth, but escaped from it on wings fashioned by Daedalus out of wax. Daedalus is less well known than his imprudent son Icarus, who flew too close to the sun and was drowned when his wings melted; Daedalus himself maintained a more judicious middle course between sea and sky and made good his escape. The myth of Daedalus provides a repertoire of symbols which are alluded to repeatedly throughout *A Portrait of the Artist as a Young Man*; on the one hand, there is flight, height, and rapture, on the other, fall (into water or mire), corruption, and capture. Stephen's moments of victory and vision are accompanied by images of soaring upward flight, from the school caps flung spinning into the air at the news of Stephen's moral victory over Father Dolan (*P.* 59), to the birds that fill him with ecstasy on the steps of the National Library (*P.* 224–5). Late in the book, Stephen identifies himself clearly and self-consciously with the person of Daedalus:

> Now, at the name of the fabulous artificer, he seemed to hear the noise of dim waves and to see a winged form flying above the waves and slowly climbing the air. What did it mean? Was it a quaint device opening a page of some medieval book of prophecies and symbols, a hawk-like man flying sunward above the sea, a prophecy of the end he had been born to serve and had been following through the mists of childhood and boyhood, a symbol of the artist forging anew in his workshop out of the sluggish matter of the earth a new soaring impalpable imperishable being? (*P.* 195)

45

Set against the kind of etherial image found at the end of this passage is a series of images of sluggish constriction or engulfment by the earth. These begin with Stephen's experience of being shouldered into the ditch as a boy at Clongowes, an experience that is returned to repeatedly – for example, in Stephen's response to the appearance of the dripping that he is devouring at the beginning of chapter 5, moments after one of his most intense visions of poetic beauty: 'The yellow dripping had been scooped out like a boghole and the pool under it brought back to his memory the dark turfcoloured water of the bath at Clongowes' (P. 200). A reading attentive to such patterns of symbolism – and there have been many such – can disclose variations upon this Daedalian pattern at almost every point in the book, right down to the innocuous-seeming football encountered on its second page, with the flight of the 'greasy leather orb . . . like a heavy bird through the grey light' suggesting a Daedalian compromise between weight and height. It is clear that the permutational instinct that Joyce displays in *Ulysses* is already well developed in *A Portrait of the Artist as a Young Man*.

At the same time, there is a danger in readings that insist too much upon such symbolic schemes, or allow them to become substituted for the work of reading the book. The danger is that of construing the book too literally as it might be manifested to the completed self-consciousness of Stephen Daedalus, or in terms of the Thomist qualities of integrity, consonance, and clarity he defines:

> Temporal or spatial, the esthetic image is first luminously apprehended as selfbounded and selfcontained upon the immeasurable background of space or time which is not it. You apprehend it as *one* thing. You see it as one whole. You apprehend its wholeness. That is *integritas*. . . . You apprehend it as balanced part against part within its limits; you feel the rhythm of its structure. . . . you apprehend it as complex, multiple, divisible, made up of its parts, the result of its parts and their sum, harmonious. That is *consonantia*. (P. 239–40)

Stephen is here describing, not a work of art, but an 'esthetic image' (whatever that is exactly). For Stephen, the aim of the work of art is to transform every appearance into the conditions spoken of by Thomas Aquinas, and, indeed, to apprehend a similar integrity and consonance in the work that he makes of his own life. But the text also appears to warn against the imposition of the static or timeless values that are here evoked. It marks out a repeated rhythm of exaltation followed by disruption and disillusion, in which the Daedalian climb into the air never finally escapes the gravitational pull of corruption. Every spiritual revelation in the book, whether sexual, religious, or artistic, is liable to relapse – *sauter pour mieux reculer*:

> An ecstasy of flight made radiant his eyes and wild his breath and tremulous and wild and radiant his windswept limbs.
> – One! Two! . . . Look out!
> – Oh, Cripes, I'm drownded!
>
> (*P.* 195)

The ideal aesthetic of self-completion which can be seen embodied in the novel is itself subject to criticism within it, in the ironic account of Stephen's vision of the redeemed world during his phase of religious conversion:

> Gradually, as his soul was enriched with spiritual knowledge, he saw the whole world forming one vast symmetrical expression of God's power and love. Life became a divine gift for every moment and sensation of which, were it even the sight of a single leaf hanging on the twig of a tree, his soul should praise and thank the Giver. The world for all its solid substance and complexity no longer existed for his soul save as a theorem of divine power and love and universality. So entire and unquestionable was this sense of the divine meaning in all nature granted to his soul that he could scarcely understand why it was in any way necessary that he should continue to live. (*P.* 175)

The excess of correspondence in this vision, the total knowledge it seems to offer of the absolute reciprocity of the microcosm and the macrocosm, constitutes the work's warning to itself against any such completed synopsis of relations. Such a view would always have turned the work of reading and rereading, a work in which author, character, and reader themselves participate, into a completed work, a form that, to the precise degree that it was specifiable apart from the details of the rereading itself, would be false and imprisoning.

This is to say more than that *A Portrait of the Artist as a Young Man* offers only conditional approval of the artistic ambitions of the later Stephen, or allows an ironically disapproving reading to flourish alongside an approving one. It is to suggest that the very equation of the work of reading with the quasi-aesthetic work of making one's soul is here subject to a paradox. The Minoan labyrinth from which Daedalus escapes, we recall, was fabricated by himself. *A Portrait of the Artist as a Young Man* refuses to separate the two attributes of aeronaut and artificer that are associated in the figure of Daedalus, and suggests that the very manner in which Stephen comes to liberating knowledge of the unity-in-multiplicity of his life is itself the formation of a kind of labyrinth; the 'workshop' in which Stephen plans to fashion the transformation of sluggish earth into spirit is the labyrinth itself. The idea of the work of the soul as an extrication of the self from what is alien to it, and an elaboration – literally, a 'working-out' – of what is authentic in and proper to it, encounters in A *Portrait of the Artist as a Young Man* a multiplicity of relations, or recollections and anticipations, of equivalences and differences, the unsummarizable totality of the work's work on itself, which goes beyond any attempt to gather it together in the closed and marketable form of a completed work. Seen in this way, the closure and completeness achieved in *A Portrait of the Artist as a Young Man* must not only be subject to, but also include within itself, those continued rereadings constituted by *Ulysses* and the rest of Joyce's work. The escape from the labyrinth offered by *A Portrait of the Artist as a Young Man* is thus in the end a kind of escape from the fantasy of escape, and the paralysing postures of fantasy that it induces. Just as Joyce himself left Ireland in order the better to reconstitute it, so we can read the eastward, outward movement of Stephen Daedalus into Europe and futurity as equivalent to the westward, inward movement of Gabriel Conroy into Ireland and history. The principle of aesthetic autonomism that Joyce began to acknowledge in the work of making a self carried out in *A Portrait of the Artist as a Young Man* was to lead, not to the mutually reinforcing and completed unity of the work, the life, and the nation, but to a much more radical conception and exemplification of the process of work itself.

4

'Literature &': *Ulysses*

Having secured Stephen's flight from Dublin at the end of *A Portrait of the Artist as a Young Man*, Joyce shows him at the beginning of *Ulysses* returned to Dublin from Paris, undiminished in ambition and discontent, but temporarily rebuffed, and more than ever fearful of engulfment by the demands of family, religion, and state. Stephen has been called home to the deathbed of his mother but has refused to kneel to pray for her soul; he will brood upon this all through Thursday, 16 June, the day on which the events of *Ulysses* take place. But if *A Portrait of the Artist as a Young Man* hints that Stephen's flight was part of, even an expression of, his immurement in the labyrinth of his own making, *Ulysses* will attempt a different kind of escape, or escape in a different direction; this time, it will appear, the artist must flee inwards, *into* the labyrinth. Instead of a clarity and integrity of soul achieved by subtraction from the mire of complexity and contingency, *Ulysses* offers us a movement towards aggregation and inclusiveness. As many have suggested, the book may be seen as a demonstration of Stephen's claim that he will transform the base matter of everyday life into art, for, where *A Portrait of the Artist as a Young Man* is singularly short of such base matter, *Ulysses* is thickly crammed with it. *A Portrait of the Artist as a Young Man* was sustained by the desire to produce and sustain patterns of opposition, between the soul of Stephen and that from which it emerges. *Ulysses* is driven by the restless interpenetration of contraries. The most diversified of these contraries are the two central characters of the book, the young artist, Stephen Dedalus and the middle-aged canvasser of advertisements, Leopold Bloom. The significance of their meeting, in the seventeenth chapter of the book, is that it appears to represent the coming-together of art and commerce, idealism and realism, individualism and civic belonging, the spirit and the body, the son and the father, the exile and the inhabitant, the making of the soul and the making of a living.[1]

These encounters are not merely the subject of *Ulysses*, for the book implicates its own form in such commingling of opposites. In engineering the encounter of the artist and the citizen, *Ulysses* also engineers its own encounter with the objects, processes, and energies of modern urban life. *Ulysses* pits modernism against modernity – defining a particular style or artistic stance which emphasizes the transcending consummation of the work of art against the ephemeral complexities of urban commerce and consumption. The story of the meeting of Stephen and Bloom which occupies much of *Ulysses* may thus be seen as a displacement into the level of content of the larger story of the encounter of the artistic Work with the work of everyday life.

This encounter has been prepared for in a neatly comical and, as it appears, peculiarly premonitory scene at the end of the surviving portion of *Stephen Hero*, in which Stephen discusses career prospects with the worldly Cranly. Cranly, who has earlier announced that he might become a pork butcher, teases Stephen with the idea: 'Would you not think of it? You could wrap your sausages in your love-poems' (*SH* 197). The ironic conjuncture of poetry and the porcine body, as well as the uncharacteristically genial attitude towards the conjuncture displayed in the narrative, look forward with strange exactitude to the early chapters of *Ulysses*, which set the anguished creative cogitations of Stephen Dedalus on Sandymount Strand against Bloom setting off to buy his pork kidney from the butcher. In its portrayal of Cranly, this portion of *Stephen Hero* seems closer to the expansive comic spirit of *Ulysses* than to the more enclosed *A Portrait of the Artist as a Young Man*. In the newsbill which Stephen and Cranly pause to read, it also gives us a verbal picturing of the meeting of styles of life and writing which *Stephen Hero* envisages in the abstract, and which *Ulysses* embodies concretely in its own process:

EVENING TELEGRAPH

NATIONALIST MEETING AT BALLINROBE
IMPORTANT SPEECHES
MAIN DRAINAGE SCHEME
BREEZY DISCUSSION
DEATH OF A WELL-KNOWN SOLICITOR
MAD COW AT CABRA
LITERATURE &

(*SH* 197)

Stephen is here threatened by the relegation of literature to the condition of a casual appendix, which apparently ranks even lower in terms of commercial pull than the item about the mad cow at Cabra; but, momentarily, the narration of *Stephen Hero* appears to part company with its hero, in its enjoyment of the comic incongruity of art and the quotidian which Stephen himself feels as a threat of debasement or engulfment. The open-ended formula 'Literature &' anticipates that calculated exposure of literature to all its various discursive antagonists and exteriors that *Ulysses* is to undertake.

The setting in which Stephen and Bloom are first brought together in *Ulysses* is, appropriately enough, the newspaper office occupied jointly by the *Freeman's Journal* and the *Evening Telegraph*, 'IN THE HEART OF THE HIBERNIAN METROPOLIS', as the opening words of the chapter have it. It is noon. Bloom has been brought there by the chance of placing an advertisement on behalf of Alexander Keyes, a tea merchant; Stephen has promised earlier in the day to use his connections to ensure publication in the paper of a letter from his employer, Mr Garrett Deasy, about an outbreak of foot-and-mouth disease among Irish cattle. The newspaper office is an appropriate meeting-place of literature and commerce; and, in the schema of relationships and correspondences that Joyce drew up for *Ulysses*, the dominating art of the chapter is said to be 'rhetoric', which exists similarly at the intersection of language and social life, or the wordy and worldy.

Indeed, there seems to be a similar play of identification and rivalry between the modernist novel and the newspaper as such, a play which summarizes the relationship of modernism and modernity. The contrasts between the form of *Ulysses* and that of the newspaper are obvious enough. *Ulysses* offers itself as the transfiguration of ordinary life, a lifting of the ephemeral into universality and permanence. Newspapers might appear, by contrast, both to represent and to be caught up in all the hurry and impermanence of modern life. If *Ulysses* represents the life of the word, newspapers represent words reduced to the deathly condition of pure materiality. As Bloom enters the newspaper office, one of the parodic headlines in the chapter announces 'THE DISSOLUTION OF A MOST RESPECTED DUBLIN BURGESS' (*U.* 98; 7. 78–9), and is followed by Bloom's reflections on the relations between the decomposing machinery of death and the machinery that composes the account of Patrick Dignam's funeral an hour or so previously: 'This morning the remains of the late Mr Patrick Dignam. Machines. Smash a man to atoms if they got him caught. Rule the world today. His machineries are pegging away too. Like these, got out of hand: fermenting' (*U.* 98; 7. 81–3). The deathliness of modern communications media is a proliferative, or fermenting, deathliness; this insight anticipates the centrality in *Finnegans Wake* of the motif of a letter buried within the fermenting litter of a compost heap. As opposed to the quasi-divine Word of the achieved modernist text, the printed words of the newspaper are disposable and easily dispersed: standing in the office of the *Freeman's Journal*, Bloom describes the design that his client wants for his advertisement, and reflects on the uses of newspaper: 'Mr Bloom . . . saw the foreman's sallow face . . . and beyond the obedient reels feeding in huge webs of paper. Clank it. Clank it. Miles of it unreeled. What becomes of it after? O, wrap up meat, parcels; various uses, thousand and one things' (*U.* 99; 7. 132–6). Bloom has himself put a newspaper to a similar use earlier in the day – the pork kidney which he carries home from Dlugacz's for his breakfast being a comic travesty of Cranly's suggestion about Stephen's use of literature to wrap sausages.

A little later, Bloom stands watching the typesetter distributing the type from the block in which it has been set. The fact that the typesetter must read the type backwards, and that what he is reading, or what Bloom imagines he is reading, is the name of the deceased Patrick Dignam, reminds Bloom of his father reading the Hebrew text of the Haggadah at Passover from right to left, an association which leads once again to thoughts of death, since the memory of Bloom's father is always associated with the memory of his suicide. So the newspaper type has been suggested as the mirror image of *Ulysses* – literally, because it is a textual decomposition of the novel being composed around it, and metaphorically, because of the association between such textual inversion and the dissolution of identity in death which its headline announces.

And yet the novel also borrows from and identifies with the practices of the typesetter. The dissolution of meaning in the newspaper office yields resources of meaning to the novel – for example, in the fact that, spelt backwards, the name of Patrick Dignam (who is, in the words of Buck Mulligan, Stephen's mocking cohabitee in the first chapter of the novel, 'beastly dead') becomes 'mangiD kcirtaP' (*U.* 101. 7. 206), which is perhaps on the way to becoming 'mangy creature', just as Patrick Dignam will himself be transformed into a dog in the 'Circe' chapter. Throughout the 'Aeolus' chapter, the play between composition and decomposition, writing and unwriting, between meaningful language and the sheets of waste paper that whirl and flutter in the destructive wind that blows through the chapter, is turned into a kind of metabolic or respiratory rhythm, in which the very alternation of forwards and backwards is turned into a principle of life.

Death features also in an advertisement which has earlier sprung to Bloom's eye in the fifth chapter of the novel and gathers a sinister force throughout the day:

> He unrolled the newspaper baton idly and read idly:
>
> > *What is home without*
> > *Plumtree's Potted Meat?*
> > *Incomplete.*
> > *With it an abode of bliss.*
>
> (*U.* 61; 5. 143–7)

The 'potted meat' of the advertisement suggests itself as a reference to the fact that Bloom and his wife have not enjoyed full sexual relations for some time, and to the irruption into the home of Blazes Boylan's virile sexuality; but the unfortunate placing of the advertisement near the deaths column of the newspaper (Bloom is looking for the time of the funeral of Patrick Dignam, which he must attend later in the morning) also suggests to Bloom an association between 'potted meat' and death. Interestingly the 'potted meat' of Patrick Dignam is itself subject to a typographical decomposition in the 'Ithaca' chapter, which echoes and extends the sequence established by the typesetter's 'mangiD kcirtaP': 'The name on the label is Plumtree. A plumtree in a meat-pot, registered trade mark. Beware of imitations. Peatmot. Trumplee. Moutpat. Plamtroo' (*U.* 560; 17. 603–5). The incompleteness of Bloom's home life is here not merely suggested by the newspaper, but in some sense enacted in the arbitrariness and incompleteness of its manner of conveying information, in the orts and scraps delivered to the idly preoccupied glance rather than free-standing works designed to elicit acts of exclusive attention. Newspapers are incomplete, because – unlike Joyce's novel – they are wholly temporal, produced in a race against time, and vulnerable to, even consumed by, it. Newspapers are an image of the restless time-consciousness of modern life in the fact that they are surrendered for almost immediate consumption, and therefore always on the point of becoming out of date; the letter, to borrow again the pun upon which much will depend in *Finnegans Wake*, is always being transformed into litter.

It is perhaps for this reason that newspapers are associated so insistently with waste and disposability throughout *Ulysses*. One of the central events of the day, Bloom's unwitting transmission of a tip for the Ascot Gold Cup in the course of a casual encounter on the street in chapter 5, revolves around just such an association:

> - I want to see about that French horse that's running today, Bantam Lyons said. Where the bugger is it?
>
> He rustled the pleated pages, jerking his chin on his high collar. Barber's itch. Tight collar he'll lose his hair. Better leave him the paper and get shut of him.
>
> – You can keep it, Mr Bloom said.
>
> – Ascot. Gold cup. Wait, Bantam Lyons muttered. Half a mo. Maximum the second.
>
> – I was just going to throw it away, Mr Bloom said.
>
> Bantam Lyons raised his eyes suddenly and leered weakly.
>
> – What's that? his sharp voice said.
>
> – I say you can keep it, Mr Bloom answered. I was going to throw it away that moment.

Bantam Lyons doubted an instant, leering; then thrust the outspread sheets back on Mr Bloom's arms.

– I'll risk it, he said. Here, thanks.

(*U.* 70; 5. 526–41)

Bloom here does not succeed in throwing away the paper, but does unconsciously throw off the hint to Bantam Lyons about the 20–1 outsider, Throwaway, which did in actual fact win the Ascot Gold Cup run on 16 June 1904. If newspapers are the consumptional unconscious of the modern city, the spasmodic passage of signs and meanings which are always on the point of being lost or forgotten, *Ulysses* is the textual memory which rescues and preserves their significance. At the same time, of course, *Ulysses* borrows and is built around the mode of attention embodied in the newspaper; the manner in which characters read newspapers, or read other texts in the mode of newspapers, establishes the material conditions for the interior monologues which represent the most well-known stylistic innovation of *Ulysses*. The interior monologues in the novel, and especially those of Leopold Bloom which dominate it, are not the mere passive registering of impressions, or the ungoverned slide of feelings; rather they are characterized by a fluid interchange of inner and outer, of private associations and external stimulus. In the passage from the 'Lotus-Eaters' episode, for example, in which Bloom encounters C. P. McCoy, we see Bloom in rapid succession, listening to McCoy recounting how he has heard of the death of Paddy Dignam, looking with interest at a handsome woman standing across the street and reflecting on her destination as she drives away in a cab, scanning the newspaper, and remembering Molly in bed, while snatches of music-hall songs run through his head (*U.* 60–1; 5. 110–61). Pages such as these bear out amply the truth of Sheldon Brivic's observation that 'every perception that appears in [Joyce's] work is an interception'.[2] The newspaper provides a kind of model for this mobile, collective archive of memories, ideas, and idioms. Because it is a shared form, the newspaper is connected to a network of knowledge and communication, which is secret and public at once, and which ramifies beyond the conscious grasp or control of individuals. Like the elaborate underground communication system or conspiracy known as W.A.S.T.E uncovered by Oedipa Maas in Thomas Pynchon's *The Crying of Lot 49*, the newspaper points in *Ulysses* to a mysterious textual economy whose purpose is to process detritus into meaning, and meaning into detritus. Seen in this way, the newspaper is not the textual adversary of the novel, but its secret model.

The association of the newspaper with waste and disposability recurs throughout *Ulysses*. At the beginning of the 'Lestrygonians' chapter, Bloom is given a handbill, or 'throwaway', announcing the arrival in Dublin of an American evangelist. After having scanned it quickly, Bloom duly throws away the throwaway off O'Connell bridge. However, like Bloom's other throwaway, his unwitting allusion to the horse of that name, it keeps coming back in the novel; its progress downstream on the Liffey is monitored through the 'Wandering Rocks' chapter, and the 'Elijah' whose coming is announced in the handbill actually makes an appearance in 'Circe'. Newspapers are associated also with bodily excess and excrescence. Stephen tears off a slip from the bottom of Mr Deasy's letter to the newspaper to write his poem on Sandymount Strand in the 'Proteus' episode (*U*. 3. 404–5), giving Myles Crawford, the editor of the *Freeman's Journal*, the opportunity to jeer 'Who tore it? Was he short taken?' (*U*. 109; 7. 521). A more extended association between newspapers and bodily evacuation is established at the end of the 'Calypso' chapter, in which Bloom picks up an old copy of *Titbits*, a popular weekly journal, to take to the lavatory with him. The pleasant rhythm of retention and release is synchronized with his reading of the story *Matcham's Masterstroke*:

> Quietly he read, restraining himself, the first column and, yielding but resisting, began the second. Midway, his last resistance yielding, he allowed his bowels to ease themselves quietly as he read, reading still patiently that slight constipation of yesterday quite gone. (*U*. 56; 4. 506–9)

Bloom's lavatory reading prompts in him a flicker of artistic ambition – 'Might manage a sketch. By Mr and Mrs L. M. Bloom' (*U*. 56; 4. 518). The fact that he ends his reading by tearing a page out of the story and wiping himself with it recurs during a guilty hallucination in the brothel later that night, when Philip Beaufoy, the author of the story, appears accusing Bloom of plagiarism, and exhibiting the stained sheet of newspaper as 'the *corpus delicti*, my lord, a specimen of my maturer work, disfigured by the hallmark of the beast' (*U*. 375; 15. 843–5), and prompting a disembodied voice to cry out 'Moses, Moses, King of the jews | Wiped his arse in the *Daily News*' (*U*. 375; 15. 847–8).

The association between Bloom's bodily products and *Titbits* also surfaces in the 'Circe' chapter in a memory of being taken short, in Myles Crawford's phrase, in the street, and having to use a plasterer's bucket as a receptacle. The chapter renders the memory in a report of Bloom's responses to interrogation:

> *The crossexamination proceeds re Bloom and the bucket. A large bucket. Bloom himself. Bowel trouble. In Beaver street. Gripe, yes. Quite bad. A plasterer's bucket. By walking stifflegged. Suffered untold misery. Deadly agony. About noon. Love or burgundy. Yes, some spinach. Crucial moment. He did not look in the bucket. Nobody. Rather a mess. Not completely. A* Titbits *back number.* (*U*. 378; 15. 929–34)

While these references amount to a mocking Stephen Dedalus-like rejection by the novel of the products of popular culture, they also express a Bloomian assimilation of them. Stanislaus Joyce records that his brother wrote at least one story in early youth which he hoped would be published in *Titbits*, and suggests that the phrases from *Matcham's Masterstroke* which are reproduced in the description of Bloom reading on the lavatory are actually taken from Joyce's own story (now lost).[3] If this is so, then *Ulysses* is at least partly identifying itself with the cultural 'other' from which it appears to distance itself; expelling the popular as so much waste and excrescence, it nevertheless identifies itself as the book in which the physical process of expulsion becomes central. The narrowly economic measure of profit in journalism (before reading the story Bloom calculates rapidly how much Philip Beaufoy has made from it – 'Payment at the rate of one guinea a column has been made to the writer. Three and a half. Three pounds three. Three pounds thirteen and six' (*U*. 56; 4. 503–5)) is drawn into the larger stylistic economy of *Ulysses*, as the economics of literary work are drawn into the economic structure of the modernist work.

The expulsion and assimilation of the language of popular culture, and especially journalistic literature, must be understood in the context of the much more general corporealization of language and style throughout *Ulysses*. Joyce told Frank Budgen that he was planning to make *Ulysses* an 'epic of the human body', and, in the 'somatic scheme of the whole' that he drew up for the novel, provided a table of organs or parts of the body which are dominant in each of the chapters.[4] Thus, for example, 'Calypso', which begins with ingestion and ends with defecation, is governed by the kidney; 'Lestrygonians', in which Bloom copes with the impulses of hunger at lunchtime, by the oesophagus; 'Aeolus', which involves much rhetorical ventilation and general windbaggery, is governed by the lungs (Joyce's fulfilment, perhaps, of the promise of the headline promising 'A Breezy Discussion' seen by Stephen and Cranly in *Stephen Hero*); the 'Sirens' episode, which is dominated by music, as Bloom sits in the Ormond Hotel bar and listens to the singing of Ben Dollard and Simon Dedalus, is organized around aurality and the ear. Joyce emphasized that he wanted not only to give an emblematic representation of the body in his novel, but to enact the living process of that body at work. He told Frank Budgen that the only other writer he knew who had attempted something similar had been the seventeenth-century poet Giles Fletcher, in his long allegorical poem about the human body, *The Purple Island*, but had gone on to contrast Fletcher's writing of the body with his own in *Ulysses*:

> His *Purple Island* is purely descriptive, a kind of coloured anatomical chart of the human body. In my book the body lives in and moves through space and is the home of a full human personality. The words I write are adapted to express first one of its functions then another.[5]

Joyce brought about this living enactment of bodily process, not just by a multiplication of references to the body (his description of Bloom on the lavatory succeeded in shocking even the otherwise zappily imperturbable Ezra Pound), but also by a stylistic imitation of bodily process – for example, in the famous respiratory pair of sentences at the beginning of 'Aeolus', which appear first to draw breath, and then slowly to let it out again: 'Grossbooted draymen rolled barrels dullthudding out of Prince's stores and bumped them up on the brewery float. On the brewery float bumped dullthudding barrels rolled by grossbooted draymen out of Prince's stores' (*U.* 96; 7. 21–4). This is recapitulated, as we have already seen, by the alternation of forwards and backwards typography in the chapter, as well as in the palindromes later perpetrated by Lenehan ('Madam I'm Adam. And Able was I ere I saw Elba' (*U.* 113; 7. 683)).

But the 'somatic scheme' of *Ulysses* involves more than references to, or evocations of, the body, frequent as these are. It also develops what we might see as the metabolic relationship between the styles of the chapters, and the styles that begin to multiply within them. As we have seen, Joyce had exploited the analogy between stylistic and physical growth in *Dubliners* and *A Portrait of the Artist as a Young Man*, both of which parallel the growth of a single consciousness, whether actual, as in *A Portrait of the Artist as a Young Man*, or virtual, as in *Dubliners*, with the movement of its style from the linguistic unconsciousness of the child in 'The Sisters' to the oratorical self-consciousness of Gabriel. Joyce developed this gestatory analogy in *Ulysses* as well, most notably in the 'Oxen of the Sun' chapter, which brings Stephen and Bloom together at a maternity hospital in Holles Street, where the stages of growth and delivery of the baby of a Mrs Purefoy are represented by a series of parodies (of variable quality) of English literature from its Anglo-Saxon beginnings through to the then present. But where the principle that I have been calling mimetic autonomism is harnessed in Joyce's earlier works to the forming and expression of a single consciousness, in *Ulysses* the principle is hugely enlarged. In *Ulysses*, the individual styles of Stephen, Bloom, Molly, and the other characters whose interior monologues the book allows us to overhear exist in an ever more complex interchange, and sometimes conflict with other, more public or impersonal styles, idioms, and voices.

Most critics of the novel would seem to agree that the expressive function of style is really sustained only up to the end of chapter 6. Up to that point, it is possible to account for nearly every stylistic peculiarity or aberration in one of two ways. It can be explained as a direct imitation of the quality of perception or affective 'style' of a particular character, whether in Stephen's learned, histrionic introspection, or in Bloom's terser, more outward-directed reflections, or it can evidence the stylistic influence exerted more obliquely upon third-person narrative by the proximity of one or other principal character. Even the dense and demandingly allusive 'Proteus' chapter, which is full of puzzling interpolations and abrupt switches of style and register, can be accounted for mimetically as a more or less exact imitation of Stephen's own versatile, linguistically invaded consciousness, which teems with Aristotelian metaphysics, scraps of conversation, symbolist poetry, and obscure Romany dialect. But, from the seventh chapter of the novel onwards, the 'Aeolus' chapter set in the newspaper room, things become progressively less easy to account for in terms of the mimesis of character. In 1921 Joyce returned to the text of the chapter, which had already been published some years previously in the *Little Review*, and began to recast it. The principal change involved the insertion of the headlines which now form so conspicuous a part of the chapter.[6] These must be regarded as the impersonal voice of the setting or physical context of the chapter, an enactment of the principle that Bloom articulates to himself as he sees and hears the automatic delivery of a batch of folded newspapers: 'Sllt. Almost human the way it sllt to call attention. Doing its level best to speak . . . Everything speaks in its own way' (*U*. 100; 7. 175–7). These headlines cannot be attributed to a single consciousness or point of view, since they comment in different ways on the segments of narrative to which they are affixed. Sometimes the headlines appear or affect to be neutral résumés of the material that follows: 'NOTED CHURCHMAN AN OCCASIONAL CONTRIBUTOR' (*U*. 100; 7. 178–9); 'MEMORABLE BATTLES RECALLED' (*U*. 105; 7. 358). Sometimes they are attempts at classical ornamentation: 'THE GRANDEUR THAT WAS ROME', (*U*. 108; 7. 483); 'ÓMNIUM GATHERUM' (*U*. 111; 7. 605); 'ITALIA, MAGISTRA ARTIUM' (*U*. 115; 7. 754). Sometimes they seem designed to transform what follows into a piece of serialized fiction: 'A DISTANT VOICE' (*U*. 112; 7. 657), 'RHYMES AND REASONS' (*U*. 114; 7. 713); 'OMINOUS – FOR HIM!' (*U*. 118; 7. 871). By the end of the chapter, when they begin to imitate the particular style of telegrammatic verbosity still exhibited by mass circulation American newspapers, the headlines pull more and more against the style and content of the bits of the narrative they designate: 'DAMES DONATE DUBLIN'S CITS SPEEDPILLS VELOCITOUS AEROLITHS, BELIEF' (*U*. 121; 7. 1021–2); 'SOPHIST WALLOPS HAUGHTY HELEN SQUARE ON PROBOSCIS. SPARTANS

GNASH MOLARS. ITHACANS VOW PEN IS CHAMP' (*U*. 122; 7. 1032–4); 'DIMINISHED DIGITS PROVE TOO TITILLATING FOR FRISKY FRUMPS. ANNE WIMBLES, FLO WANGLES – YET CAN YOU BLAME THEM?' (*U*. 123; 7.1069–71). Their purpose seems to be not simply to translate the material of the narrative into 'journalese', but rather to exploit the fact that a newspaper is itself a stylistic compound, or 'omnium gatherum', of styles, with no consistent author, purpose, or attitude.

Many of the chapters of *Ulysses* seem to be governed by the principle of stylistic competition. Often it is as though, rather than giving expression to a consciousness, the styles of the chapters represent alien threats to or potential distortions of, that consciousness. Thus, in the 'Lestrygonians' chapter, Bloom's hunger appears to swamp his thoughts and feelings with an uncharacteristic oral rage, against which he must struggle to regain his natural equipoise. Similarly, in 'Hades', Bloom must fight off the sentimental morbidity that surrounds him in the funeral party and threatens to overtake his own thoughts. The consuming temptation of different forms of sentimentality is enacted in the 'Sirens' chapter in the music that Bloom hears, and the musical form into which the writing of this chapter casts his thoughts, as well as in the 'Nausicaa' chapter, in which the style of Gerty's imputed monologue, which Joyce described to Frank Budgen as a 'namby-pamby jammy marmalady drawersy . . . style with effects of incense, mariolatry, masturbation, stewed cockles, painter's palette, chitchat, circumlocutions, etc etc' (*L*. i. 135), seems at the climactic moment of the chapter, when Bloom ejaculates at the sight of Gerty showing him her knickers, to cross over telepathically, or, shall we say, tele-idiomatically, to Bloom himself. In the 'Cyclops' chapter, the stylistic threat is much less internalized, and correspondingly much more brutal, as the narrow-minded, violent nationalism of the Citizen is expressed in a series of extravagant, or, to use Joyce's own word from his schema for the novel, 'gigantist', forms of over-writing, literary and journalistic, against which Bloom must take a risky ethical stand. In 'Circe' both Bloom and Stephen suffer from the combined effects of guilt, drunkenness, and sexual delusion, which not only take over the style of the chapter, but seem to bring about ghostly materializations for each of the characters,

Stephen seeing the ghost of his dead mother, Bloom the ghost of his dead grandfather and dead son.

All of the stylistic excesses, invasions, and distortions in these chapters seem to require some discharge from the 'body textual' of the book, in order that balanced functioning may be restored. Bloom is subject to the influence of Philip Beaufoy only for the period that he spends on the lavatory; the process of defecation over, he emerges 'from the gloom into the air', not only 'lightened and cooled in limb' (*U*. 57; 4. 539–41), but relieved of the oppression of Philip Beaufoy's stylistic banality. When Bloom farts at the end of 'Sirens', when he ejaculates in 'Nausicaa', or when his trouser button pings off in 'Circe' at the end of a consuming sentimental fantasy of ideal womanly beauty, precipitating the cracking apart of the image of the Nymph which hangs over the Blooms' bed, '*a cloud of stench escaping from the cracks*' (*U*. 451; 15. 3470), the effect is to restore a linguistic balance that is consonant with the physiological balance of his internal processes. Style in *Ulysses* must be seen, therefore, not as expressive but as dynamic – not as the gradual unfolding of an interior essence of selfhood, but rather as a ceaseless metabolic interchange of self and other, intimate and alien, internal and external.

All this might nevertheless suggest that the extended analogy between body and language in *Ulysses* is intended to build towards a complete and harmonious discursive physiology. Joyce's own remarks about his epic of the body, along with the various versions he provided of the schema for the novel, with their careful coordination of language, rhetoric, and physical process, certainly seem to suggest that he had something like this in mind. But we should also note the influence of a powerfully contrary tendency in the novel, which permits, even insists on, the principles of hypertrophic expansion and overflow, both in stylistic and bodily terms, over the principles of balance and the harmonious cooperation of parts. From 'Aeolus' onwards, as many have noticed, the tendency is for the style(s) of each chapter to engorge massively, until they occupy the whole field of the reader's attention. Added to this is the tendency for each chapter to draw the rest of the novel into itself, a tendency which resists the subordination of each chapter to the overall scheme. 'Aeolus' is the first chapter in *Ulysses* which we can take as a mimesis not only of a particular time and place, or the expression of a particular 'organ' in the composite stylistic body of the text (to borrow the pun which features in the chapter itself, in the headline 'HOW A GREAT DAILY ORGAN IS TURNED OUT' (*U*. 98; 7. 84)), but of the quality and structure of *Ulysses* itself. Some of the headlines even seem like potential titles for other chapters in the novel. 'A STREET CORTEGE' (*U*. 107; 7. 443) might neatly name the 'Hades' chapter, and 'SPOT THE WINNER' (*U*. 105; 7. 386) would fit with 'Lotus Eaters', in which Bloom unwittingly tips the horse Throwaway. 'IN THE HEART OF THE HIBERNIAN METROPOLIS' (*U*. 96; 7. 1–2) would do pretty well as a title for the 'Wandering Rocks', while the 'Sirens' chapter, which is built around the rhythm of Bloom's gathered and released flatulence, is evoked by 'RAISING THE WIND' (*U*. 121; 7. 995). Taken together, the consecutive headlines 'A COLLISION ENSUES' and 'EXIT BLOOM' (*U*. 106; 7. 414, 7. 429), point forward to the ending of the 'Cyclops' chapter, in which Bloom exits hurriedly, followed by the biscuit tin thrown at him by the enraged Citizen. Bloom's homecoming in 'Ithaca' is anticipated in 'RETURN OF BLOOM' (*U*. 120; 7. 962), while the style of formal question and answer in that chapter is suggested by the interrogative headlines '???' and 'WHAT? – AND LIKEWISE – WHERE?' (*U*. 109; 7. 512, *U*. 122; 7. 1050). 'Penelope' makes an appearance in 'ITHACANS VOW PEN IS CHAMP' (*U*. 122; 7. 1034, 'Penelope') and the 'Aeolus' chapter even seems to generate an alternative name for itself in 'WE SEE THE CANVASSER AT WORK' (*U*. 99; 7. 120). From this point on in *Ulysses* the chapters are going to be less and less composed (in both senses of the word) and more and more compounded out of different, and conflicting, elements. The effect is to produce, not the idealized linguistic–stylistic body posited by Joyce's remarks to Budgen, but rather an unstable, disproportioned, incontinent, even explosive body, which is expressed in excess and discharge rather than restraint and bounding.

The manuscript evidence of Joyce's methods of composition for *Ulysses* suggest another aspect of this structural incontinence. As he approached the end of his task, with the writing of the final chapters, 'Circe', 'Eumaeus', 'Ithaca', and 'Penelope', Joyce began to review the earlier chapters which he had already written and which had sometimes already appeared in print. In the case of the 'Aeolus' chapter, as we have just seen, the result was to make a chapter which had hitherto been relatively straightforward in stylistic terms begin to resemble later chapters such as 'Sirens' and 'Circe', in the addition of the headlines, which give to the realistic setting of the newspaper office a perverse voice and pseudo-consciousness which interfere with its realistic effect. The novel that we now have is usually seen as showing a carefully deliberated progress from chapters which adhere to the conventions of novelistic realism through to the crowded, thickly interwoven later chapters, with their flamboyant display of styles and the elaborate chamberings of their *mis-en-abîme* and inter-reference; and the 'Aeolus' chapter is often held to mark the point of transition beyond realistic conventions. One of the most obvious effects of this progression is that the chapters get steadily much longer, as Joyce took the opportunity to fill them out internally with more and more digressions, expansions, and variations.

Of course, this is part of the natural process by which any book builds towards wholeness; as the unity of the design becomes apparent, authors will often turn back to the early parts of a book to draw them into concord with the whole that has emerged through its writing. What is remarkable about *Ulysses* is the degree of the transformation of the early chapters suggested by the discoveries Joyce had made in its later stages. The mode of recapitulation which characterizes the later chapters such as 'Circe' and 'Ithaca', which obsessively recycle and recast events, conversations, and ideas from earlier in the novel, begins to be matched by the retrospective working-over of the earlier parts of the text by the writing modes of the later. As with *A Portrait of the Artist as a Young Man*, in fact, Joyce had found a way of writing which results in a work which relentlessly works on itself. In principle, as is demonstrated by Joyce's irrepressible urge to add material even at proof stage, the writing and rewriting of *Ulysses* could have gone on indefinitely, with first thoughts and afterthoughts becoming tangled up with each other in increasingly complex feedback loops. The celebrated wholeness of the book's stylistic and thematic physiology is all the more breathtaking for being an effect of the interruption of processes that threatened to become interminable. The book came to an end, not with the working-out of its immanent purposes, but with its strategic abandonment; not with the achievement of a rational and organic 'epic body', but with the intimation of a kind of stylistic incontinence which would precipitate Joyce into the writing of *Finnegans Wake*.

Such a contrast has often been encoded in European tradition in gendered terms, which anxiously oppose the girded, rationalized male body against the allegedly unnerving fluidity of the female body. In *Ulysses*, this contrast is associated intimately with a gendering of cultural style, in which the male body is threatened by the moral-stylistic temptations of gush, hype, and obsession instanced principally in the popular literature that the book seems playfully to represent as its other, and code as female. Odd as it may seem, however, there is a close relationship between the mimsy archness of Gerty Macdowell's discourse – or, rather, the discourse of female romantic fiction that speaks itself *through* her, since she is often to be heard resisting its pull:

> A gnawing sorrow is there all the time. Her very soul is in her eyes and she would give worlds to be in the privacy of her own familiar chamber where, giving way to tears, she could have a good cry and relieve her pentup feelings though not too much because she knew how to cry nicely before the mirror . . . (*U.* 288; 13. 188–92)

and the brawny inflation of the interpolated passages in 'Cyclops', which embody imaginary newspaper reports about the discussion of Gaelic sports:

> The venerable president of the noble order was in the chair and the attendance was of large dimensions. After an instructive discourse by the chairman, a magnificent oration eloquently and forcibly expressed, a most interesting and instructive discussion of the usual high standard of excellence ensued as to the desirability of the revivability of the ancient games and sports of our ancient Panceltic forefathers. (*U.* 260; 12. 901–6)

If we see *Ulysses* as both parodically indulging and discharging these stylistic enlargements, and thus working always in the direction of moderation and equanimity, then this might again be to see the book as a modernist work, that forms itself out of the denial of the mere workings of the popular imagination, which are at once paralysed and nauseatingly proliferative. But it is hard to maintain this particular pattern consistently, given that *Ulysses* comes to identify itself with the very principles of excess and ungoverned enlargement that it also attempts to control by attributing it to the libidinal or languorous female imaginary of popular culture. The voices of Gerty Macdowell and Molly Bloom are certainly subject to comic travesty through exaggeration, but the porousness of their language, and their oddly alert passivity with regard to the ambient rhythms and idioms of popular culture, come in fact to be the dominant mode of *Ulysses*.

If *Ulysses* begins by attempting to maintain the distinction between literature and the popular culture, represented above all by the newspapers, which threatens to engulf it, and attempts, as it were, to reverse the order of priority which makes 'Literature &' merely one of the elements in the ill-assorted *mélange* of cultural items in the newsbill read by Stephen and Cranly, then the book is finally unable to resist the vitality and excessiveness of the etcetera implied after the ampersand. Literature is here unable and unwilling merely to enclose the workings of the popular against which it begins by defining itself. In the end, of course, *Ulysses* itself is able to enclose the discursive world of the newspaper only by means of an imitation of its qualities: the unity of *Ulysses* is not the Thomist *integritas* looked for by Stephen, but the complex, and unfinished commingling of incommensurables signified in the newsbill.

Ulysses begins in a tower, and ends in an earthy bed. As Yeats was proposing the tower as the symbol of the artist's soul refining itself in contradistinction to the world of political and cultural mutability, Joyce, who wrote *Ulysses*, as he did most of his works, in a condition of restless motion across European cities, was creating a text about mobility produced under highly mobile conditions. Above all, what Joyce encountered on the imaginary streets of the Dublin through which his characters pass, was a mode of that reading in public and on the move which has become so distinctive a feature of modern urban life. Scarcely ever in *Ulysses* does a character read in a classic fashion, sitting down, and in isolation from the demands and rhythms of life and work. The reading (and writing) that is done in the novel, and which perhaps proposes a model for the mobile reading of the novel, is peripatetic; Bloom reading *Titbits* on the lavatory is nevertheless surrendering himself to the physical motion of his bowels; Stephen writes on the beach with whatever comes to hand; all day, Bloom reads headlines, hoardings, and announcements in the streets; and in 'Wandering Rocks', a chapter that is overseen by the travelling discourse of the throwaway as it floats down the

Liffey, Stephen and Bloom turn over books standing up in the street. Perhaps the most emphatic embodiment of kinetic text is the chain of sandwich-men advertising Hely's stationers and printers, which first appears in the 'Lestrygonians' chapter (*U.* 127; 8. 123–6), and winds and plods its way through the streets of Dublin throughout the novel. Rather than merely including or representing the motion of words and the mobility of the reading eye, *Ulysses* seeks to identify itself with its text in motion. Bloom in fact has Stephen Dedalus-like aspirations to an art of advertisement that would reduce all movement and irrelevance to static or epiphanic form. Before retiring for the night, we are told, he thinks about the possibility of

> some one sole unique advertisement to cause passers to stop in wonder, a poster novelty, with all extraneous accretions excluded, reduced to its simplest and most efficient terms not exceeding the span of casual vision and congruous with the velocity of modern life. (*U.* 592; 17. 1770–3)

The possibility of achieving arrest for Bloom is measured in terms of the background expectation of 'casual vision' and 'the velocity of modern life'. But Bloom also recognizes the necessary mobility of the art of advertisement. Frustrated by the redundancy and bad design of the newspaper advertisements he sees during the day, he has visions of advertisement as the impermanent art of the city. He is impressed, for example, by the rowboat anchored on the Liffey which bears the legend 'Kino's 11/- Trousers' (*U.* 126; 8. 90–2), perhaps partly because of its use of the mobile element of water, for he thinks 'Wonder if he pays rent to the corporation. How can you own water really? It's always flowing in a stream, never the same' (*U.* 126; 8. 93–4). We learn that, when Bloom worked at Hely's stationers, he had an idea for an advertising stunt which would have been a spectacular enlargement of the sandwich-board men, involving a showcart drawn through the city in which smart girls would be on display writing with implements obtained from Hely's store. When Bloom conveys the idea to Stephen as they drink their cocoa in the kitchen of Bloom's house in Eccles Street during the 'Ithaca' chapter, Stephen expands it into a short scenario involving the dramatization of the curiosity which Bloom hopes to evoke:

Solitary hotel in mountain pass. Autumn. Twilight. Fire lit. In dark
corner young man seated. Young woman enters. Restless. Solitary.
She sits. She goes to window. She stands. She sits. Twilight. She
thinks. On solitary hotel paper she writes. She thinks. She writes.
She sighs. Wheels and hoofs. She hurries out. He comes from his
dark corner. He seizes solitary paper. He holds it towards fire.
Twilight. He reads. Solitary.

What?

In sloping, upright and backhands: Queen's Hotel, Queen's Hotel,
Queen's Hotel, Queen's Ho . . . (*U.* 560; 17. 612–20)

Stephen seems to have moved beyond Bloom's idea for a travelling advertisement, but preserves its kinetic nature in the
cinematic changes of focus and viewpoint that his scene requires.
This act of collaboration between the artist and the commercial
traveller enacts the travelling nature of the art of *Ulysses* itself.
Multi-voiced, even, perhaps, multi-authored, delighting in the
contiguity of the incongruous, snatched out of time, and yet, like
the newspaper, tied to time (for *Ulysses*, like the Dublin and
London newspapers for 16 June 1904 which Joyce pillaged for
his novel, is above all a 'journal', a book of a day), *Ulysses* manufactures an extraordinary *rapprochement* between the modernist
art that transcends the quotidian and a kind of art, which it
would perhaps be more proper to call postmodernist, which
inhabits it.

The literal mobility of the word in the art of advertisement
or the circulating verbal media of the metropolis connects significantly with the questions of national identity, belonging, and
displacement which are developed throughout *Ulysses*. Early in
the day, Bloom's eye is caught by an advertisement for 'Agendath
Netaim', a plantation company in Palestine, on the sheet of newspaper in which his pork kidney is wrapped. This is the first of
many associations in *Ulysses* between the instability of the word
represented in newspapers and the instability of forms of ethnic
and national belonging. Bloom, who is a Jew, though not an
orthodox or practising Jew, allows himself a daydream about
emigration to Palestine, a dream of permanence beyond change
– 'Quiet long days: pruning, ripening . . . Always the same, year
after year' (*U.* 49; 4. 202, 209) – even though he recognizes that
there is 'nothing doing' in such a prospect. In the next chapter,
Bloom will revert to this daydream, this time in thoughts of the

Far East prompted by the display in the windows of the Belfast and Oriental Tea Company – 'Those Cinghalese lobbing about in the sun in *dolce far niente*' (*U*. 58; 5. 31–2). In his dismissive 'nothing doing' of earlier in the day, Joyce allows Bloom to anticipate the *far niente* with an unconscious, wryly appropriate translation. There is 'nothing doing' for Bloom in such an image because of his sense of the fundamental mutability of the human condition, and especially of the Jewish and Irish peoples, condemned as they have both been to wandering and exile: 'A bent hag crossed from Cassidy's, clutching a naggin bottle by the neck. The oldest people. Wandered far away all over the earth, captivity to captivity, multiplying, dying, being born everywhere' (*U*. 50; 4. 224–6). The knitting-together of the dream of belonging and the condition of displacement is apparent in one final detail of the advertisement for 'Agendath Netaim', the fact that its address is given as 'Bleibtreustrasse 34, Berlin' (*U*. 49; 4. 199). Bloom is painfully aware throughout the day that he not only belongs to a displaced and unhoused people but is also being usurped in his own home – by Blazes Boylan, who commits adultery with his wife Molly. The dream of ethnic belonging is as ironically undercut as the dream of domestic harmony in the address which translates as 'Stay-true Street'.

The characters in the 'Aeolus' chapter are much concerned with the relations between nation and language; one of them, 'professor MacHugh', who is a teacher of Latin, regrets the association between that imperial language and the imperial influence of Britain: 'I teach the blatant Latin language. I speak the tongue of a race the acme of whose mentality is the maxim: time is money' (*U*. 110; 7. 555–6). The rest of the chapter balances the claims to nationhood embodied in public language against the more material pressures on language. The climax of the chapter comes with a discussion of a famous rhetorical interchange about the question of national identity during a public debate at Trinity College. For the newspapermen and their associates, rhetoric has real political force, for nationhood itself is called up and recalled in the act of language. At the same time, the chapter keeps us ironically aware of the windy vacuity of much of the political oratory in the chapter; if the utterance of the political word is a way of affirming political belonging in place, then there is also something shakily inconstant about a politics based purely on the word, and on the shiftiness and instability of verbal report, especially as it is represented by the newspaper. Professor MacHugh's re-enactment of John F. Taylor's famous rhetorical comparison of the Irish to the Jews whom Moses led out of captivity in Egypt makes Stephen think 'Gone with the wind. . . . The tribune's words, howled and scattered to the four winds. A people sheltered within his voice. Dead noise. Akasic records of all that ever anywhere wherever was' (*U.* 118; 7. 880–3). The 'Akasic records' that Stephen refers to here are a theosophical conception of the infinite memory of nature in which every experience is preserved for ever.[7] His words are framed by the two statements that establish the polarities of this chapter: 'That is oratory, the professor said uncontradicted' (*U.* 118; 7. 879) and his own blunt, unspoken assertion 'I have money' (*U.* 118; 7. 884). Interestingly, when he was given the opportunity of recording the sound of his own voice reading some of *Ulysses*, Joyce chose to read a section from MacHugh's rendering of Taylor's speech. In entrusting his own voice to the acoustic rather than the Akasic record, Joyce seems deliberately and ironically to implicate *Ulysses* itself in the oratorical impermanence, the 'dead noise', and the scattering of literature into litter, implied by the scene in the newspaper office.

The confrontation with and embrace of the newspaper in the 'Aeolus' chapter can stand for the more general self-exposure which *Ulysses* manufactures to the dangerous, fascinating forces of modernity. Modernity could be experienced as a sickening flux of forms, the forces of universal transformation – economic, psychological, technological, political – in which apparently nothing could stand firm and enduring. But it also expressed itself in forms of fixation or imaginative paralysis, such as is instanced in the bigotry of the Citizen or the exclusiveness of the various, largely male gatherings to be found in the novel. The structure of 'Cyclops', with its strange association between the brutal political rigidity of its central character, and the slipperiness of its unnamed narrator, is one instance of this compounding of fixity and impermanence. A similar compounding can be found in the 'Nausicaa' chapter, which shows the degree of Gerty MacDowell's possession by sentimental and religiose fantasy, even as it mimics the shifting and unstable nature of that fantasy: not only does Gerty move in and out of the language of romantic fiction (unless it moves in and out of her); it is also transmitted, quasi-telepathically, to Leopold Bloom. Once again, the paralysing effects of the languages and forms of consciousness associated with modern mass media are bound up paradoxically with their impermanence, and their capacity for permeation. The convulsive rhythm of the 'Circe' chapter is dominated by what Joyce described to Frank Budgen as 'the rhythm of locomotor ataxia',[8] which appears similarly to be the result of a compounding of the opposite principles of compulsive fixation and mutative flux; it is a chapter in which identities, voices, and appearances shift constantly, driven by the motor of brutalizing obsession, whether in Bloom's sadomasochistic fantasies, or in Stephen's horrified dream of the corpse of his mother rising to reproach him.

The understanding of the relations between *Ulysses* and the modern world appears to have gone through three historical stages, which mimic perhaps the three stages of art, the lyrical, epical, and dramatic, defined by Stephen in *A Portrait of the Artist as a Young Man*. The first stage covers the period of the writing and periodical publication of *Ulysses* and extends after its publication in 1922 to the beginnings of the novel's passage into critical respectability in the years following the publication of Stuart Gilbert's semi-authorized study of it.[9] This stage is characterized by baffled, negative, and hostile responses. During this period, *Ulysses* is read as a horrifying surrender or release of dark and ugly energies, energies identified both with the body and with the forms of modern life; it is said both to reveal and revel in the filth, ennui, and corruption of modern urban life.[10] A sophisticated, and aestheticized version of this criticism is to be found in Wyndham Lewis's *Time and Western Man*, which attacked the work of Joyce as representative of the decadent time-obsession of the modern Western world.[11]

The second stage in the reading of *Ulysses* extends from the 1930s through to the 1970s, and marks the critical rehabilitation of the novel. The labour of explication carried out in these years is intended to show that *Ulysses* immerses itself in the destructive element of modernity and mass culture in order precisely to transform that destructiveness into art. It is a work of critical transformation which exactly and uncannily shadows the work of spiritual–aesthetic transformation said to be undertaken in the novel. By the 1960s, *Ulysses* had been transformed from a dark and threatening exposure of, and to, the baseness and horror of modern life, into a rich and complex refusal of that modernity. Modernity here brings forth modernism.[12]

The third stage, which extends from about the 1970s to our own period, reflects the new complexity of the understanding of the relations between modernism and modernity, high and mass culture, art and the commodity, which arose during that period, especially in discussion of postmodernism. This way of reading *Ulysses*, of which this present discussion is doubtless an example, is less certain of the nature of the willed surrender to the modern brought about by, and in, the novel. Central to this way of reading *Ulysses* has been an enlarged understanding of the politics of voices, both in narrative and in social life – their origins, processes of transmission, conflicts, and forms of authority. The cultural work on modernity undertaken in *Ulysses* can thus be seen as a work of voicing. The novel anticipates its successor, *Finnegans Wake*, in beginning to use the novel form as a sounding board or receiving apparatus for the manifold voices, styles, and idioms which throng about and permeate modern subjectivity. Perhaps this reaches its point of maximum intensity in the 'Circe' chapter, which explores that condition of ventriloquial logomachia, or universal war of voices which is to be the structure of Joyce's next work, for in 'Circe', not only does everything speak 'in its own way', but everyone and everything also speaks in the way of, or through the mouths of, others. Here, Joyce presses the principle of mimetic autonomism almost beyond the power of the text to channel and contain it, forcing on us the conundrum: who speaks, when everything has a voice?

5

A *Wake* in Progress: *Finnegans Wake*

The work of *Ulysses*, far from having been completed on its appearance in 1922, had scarcely begun. In reality, the achievement of its status as a completed work would come to be dependent upon the labours of promotion, explanation, and evaluation undertaken by a couple of generations of scholars, labours which Joyce himself energetically fostered. The work would become complete only at the point at which it became available for reading, which is to say at the point at which the reader had been supplied with enough supplementary memory to be able to apprehend the structure of the work as a whole. *Ulysses* is, in perhaps rather a traditional sense, a didactic work, whose aim is the education of the reader, though that education has no moral or political aim. Indeed, perhaps it would be better to say that the work of *Ulysses* is the production of a reader, or a way of reading, that would make it possible to read the work in the first place – or the last instance, since there is no real temporal first place in which Joyce's book may be read. *Ulysses* is a work that inhabits a future perfect tense: it is a work that always *will have been* understood, in this or that manner. The reader beginning the novel is always in two places, or at two points in time; both previous and subsequent to a reading of the novel that would be adequate to it, inadequately supplied with the resources of patience, memory, and knowledge necessary to understand it and yet aware increasingly that such resources are steadily becoming available, in the form of the explicatory materials which supplement, surround, and support the work. From the very beginning, *Ulysses* proposes itself as a completable labour, as a work that can come to be read, even though that reading will require an enlargement of the notion of reading and the reader that puts pressure on the traditional idea of the self-sufficient work and its availability to the autonomous reader. *Ulysses* is the representative modernist literary work precisely because of this paradox; it is able to offer itself as a complete and all-inclusive world, a world which superbly, presumptuously subordinates the real world by assimilating it entirely to itself, but is dependent upon the work of others, the shared and progressive work of secondary understanding represented by criticism and academic study, for its plenitudinous self-identity. The heroic self-sufficiency of *Ulysses* can be achieved only under conditions of its radical dependence on the readers it seems – at least from the artificial retrospect of its perfected understanding – itself to provoke and require.

Finnegans Wake, the great work which consumed Joyce's time and labour for the seventeen remaining years of his life, appears similarly to be pledged to the aim of producing a reader adequate to itself. Here, however, we may say that the gap in time between the text and the manner of its reading shows fewer signs of being closed than in the case of *Ulysses*. We cannot say with the same confidence of *Finnegans Wake* as we can of *Ulysses* that it *will have found* its reader, or appropriate manner of reading. It unfolds repeatedly in the temporality, the temporal intrigue, of the future imperfect. *Ulysses* always was going to have become readable; not only is *Finnegans Wake* still not entirely readable, it may yet not ever succeed in becoming so. Necessarily, a guide to the reading of *Finnegans Wake* needs to take account of this sense of uncompletable, uncomprehendable work that it evokes.

But the degree of the *Wake*'s unreadability can be, and, I am convinced, regularly is, overstated. For, as with *Ulysses*, we are far from being in the same position of its first readers. The present-day reader can take advantage of the many explications of the text that have been made available in the sixty years or so since it began to appear, among which the most notable are perhaps, in roughly chronological order, the contributions of Samuel Beckett, Joseph Campbell and Henry Morton Robinson, William York Tindall, Clive Hart, Adaline Glasheen, Bernard Benstock, Danis Rose and John O'Hanlon, Roland McHugh, Margot Norris, David Hayman, and John Gordon. Although there are disagreements among these critics (how could there not be?), the very challenge of the *Wake* seems at times to cement its readers into solidarity, and there is actually far more complementarity if not actual unanimity among critics of *Finnegans Wake* as to what it consists of and how it works than is to be found in the criticism of many other texts.

I would wager that few would disagree wildly with an account of what 'happens' in the book such as the following. The first chapter opens with an evocation of the themes of rise and fall, death and resurrection, that are going to dominate the book, and introduces us to the coalescing figures of the Irish legendary hero Finn MacCool, Tim Finnegan, the bricklayer, wit, and drinker who in the music-hall song 'Finnegan's Wake' is woken from the dead by a shower of whisky spilt over him in the course of a fight that has broken out at his wake, and the figure of 'HCE', or Humphrey Chimpden Earwicker, a Dublin publican whose dream all of this might be. It will emerge that HCE is possessed of a wife, known as ALP, or Anna Livia Plurabelle, as well as two quarrelling sons, Shem and Shaun, and a daughter, called Iseult, Isolde, Isobel, or just Issy. The first chapter gives us a scene from an epical history of Ireland, which is also a history of the world, including an interpolated fairy story which appears to deal in cryptic form with the courtship of the young ALP, appearing as the teasing 'Prankquean', and HCE, disguised as 'Jarl van Hoother'. In the next chapter, HCE is described as meeting a character known as the 'cad' in Phoenix Park in Dublin, as a result of which whispers and rumours begin to circulate regarding HCE's alleged impropriety with some young girls; he has perhaps been guilty of voyeurism, or of exposing himself to them, and may have been seen by some soldiers. The next chapter extends and overlays commentary on this encounter, including one of the many lectures by a character whom some identify with Shaun. Chapter 4 begins with a meditation on the death and burial of HCE, and goes on to describe his arraignment by four judges, who will reappear at points in the book as annalists, analysts, and the four gospellers, followed by an evocation of the hunting of a fox who is probably HCE himself, and concluding with a kind of hymn to ALP and the flowing river with which she is identified. Chapter 5 describes a letter, seemingly written by ALP to HCE, and also concerning him. The letter has been found by a hen, scratching in a midden heap, and gives rise to a long, crazily dishevelled scholarly disquisition. Chapter 6 concerns the asking and answering of twelve questions, directed perhaps by Shem to Shaun. The questions concern such topics as the heraldic arms of the city of Dublin, the customers in the pub kept by HCE, and come to a climax with the digressive, highly embellished reply to a question that seems to concern Shem, a reply that evokes any number of antagonisms, philosophical, artistic, sexual, and otherwise, and includes the fable of the Mookse and the Gripes, who stand for space and time, Shaun and Shem, Wyndham Lewis (who condemned Joyce's work as symptomatic of the time-obsessed degeneracy of the modern age), and Joyce himself. This self-portrait is massively enlarged in chapter 7, which is devoted to an account of Shem, the artist, sponger, and pervert, as seen through the disapproving eyes of his more conventional brother Shaun. Chapter 8, perhaps the most well known of the book, follows the meandering talk of two wash-erwomen, as they wash the clothes of HCE and ALP on the banks of the Liffey and gossip about the alleged transgressions of HCE and his relationship with ALP. Famously, Joyce packed their speech with the names of hundreds of rivers.

The eight chapters of Book I have principally concerned HCE and ALP; Books II and III will focus much more on their children. Chapter II.1 is structured around the play of Issy, along with twenty-eight seductive girlfriends and her two brothers. We are prepared for the play at the beginning of the chapter by a theatrical handbill advertising an entertainment called 'The Mime of Mick, Nick and the Maggies'. The play involves a riddle-game, in which Shem (here designated Glugg) must guess the colour of the knickers worn by Issy. Shem twice guesses wrongly and retreats in disgusted exile, while the girls dance in admiration around his brother Chuff. The game is broken up by the arrival of HCE, calling the children in to tea. The next chapter (II.2), among the most impenetrable in the book, is an account of the lessons learnt by the children, presented in the form of a didactic text, which covers themes in grammar, rhetoric, and logic (the trivium of classical education) and arithmetic, geometry, astronomy, and music (the subsidiary quadrivium in classical education). As is often the case in the *Wake*, the academic material covers a concern with the primal narratives of the body, especially the interest of the children in procreation and parental private parts. The main text is accompanied by facetious marginalia from Shem on the left of the page, and solemnly scholarly annotations by Shaun on the right (they swap sides though not typefaces after p. 293). At the bottom of the page are breezy, teasing little footnotes from Issy. The chapter ends with a series of essay titles, and a scribbled goodnight letter from the children to their parents. The next chapter (II.3) is built around stories apparently told in the pub by HCE to his customers. The first is usually known as the story of Kersse and the Norwegian captain, or the tailor and the sailor, and is interspersed with ribald commentary from the customers in the bar, as well as snatches from a radio broadcast. HCE is called to bed by ALP, in a message delivered by the servant Kate, but he lingers, either to tell the story of Buckley the Russian general, or to watch it enacted on a television in the bar between two stand-up comics, Butt and Taff. The story, told by Butt in the first person, concerns an Irish soldier in the Crimean War who came upon a Russian general defecating, but was unable to shoot him until he saw him rip up a piece of turf with which to wipe himself. HCE delivers a monologue of self-justification to the customers in the bar, after which comes closing time. The customers weave off unsteadily, and HCE goes round draining the dregs in the glasses, until he falls down drunk. The next short chapter (II.4) gives us some confused history, rendered to us in the testimony of the four witnesses who have appeared at various points in the *Wake*. These four accounts concern not the life of Christ, but the story of the rivalry between father and son concentrated in the story of Tristan and Isolde, in which the young Tristan betrays the old King Mark by eloping with his intended bride Isolde.

The four chapters of Book III concern Shaun. In III.1 he is depicted as a postman, and it is customary for the *Wake* to contrast Shaun as the bearer of the word with Shem its artistic originator. In this, Shaun might be conflated with Bloom, who, as a canvasser of advertisements, is also an intermediary of the word, in contrast to Stephen as the artistic originator of words (though we should remember that Stephen is also the bearer of a letter in *Ulysses*). The letter that Shaun is carrying is perhaps the letter encountered in I.5. Shaun is apparently leaving Dublin, perhaps in a barrel floating down the Liffey, from which his voice emanates, responding to a series of questions and prompts with various parables and expostulations. Notable among these is another fable of brotherly conflict, the story of the Ondt and the Gracehoper, which sets the Shaun-like temperance and industry of the ant against the profligate, time-wasting Gracehoper (*FW* 414. 22–419. 10).). At the end of the chapter, Shaun in his barrel disappears from view and is lamented by his sister. In chapter III.2 we seem to be taken back a little in time. Shaun, now transmogrified into Jaun (in the next chapter he will become Yawn), is still drifting down the Liffey in his barrel, taking his leave from Dublin. He, or his barrel, comes temporarily to rest by a convent school on the banks of the river, whose pupils are Issy and her twenty consorts. Jaun launches into a long sermon, directed towards his sister, which begins with friendly advice but modulates into bullying, lubricious threats about what Jaun will do to Issy (but she now has the more *distrait* name of Tizzy) if he ever finds out that she has succumbed to the advances of any of the Shem-like Lotharios who throng his imagination. Tizzy replies, with a babytalk compliance that itself modulates into sexual titillation. At the end of the chapter, Jaun vanishes out to sea again, amid predictions of his triumphant return to Ireland.

Chapter III.3 is another inquisition, conducted, as usual, by the chorus of the four annalist–gospellers (Matthew, Mark, Luke, and John, or, collectively, 'Mamalujo'), and addressed to Shaun, as Yawn, who has collapsed into an exhausted sleep on – or perhaps in the form of – a mountain. The inquisition is part psychoanalysis, part courtroom scene, part spiritualist *séance*, and part radio broadcast, and, perhaps because Yawn is asleep, solicits the testimony of various voices which speak through him. These include the voices of his brother Shem, of ALP, defending her husband against the gossipy rumours surrounding him, of Sigurdson, or Sickerson, a police constable who has been involved in apprehending HCE in the park, of Kate, the servant in the pub, of the spirit of Oscar Wilde, and, finally, the testimony of HCE himself, in an extended piece of self-justification and self-glorification not unlike the passage celebrating Bloom's New Bloomusalem in the 'Circe' episode of *Ulysses*. Chapter III.4 suddenly switches to a much more domestic perspective. Its setting is 'interior of dwelling on outskirts of city' (*FW* 558. 36–559.1), in which the four gospellers collate descriptions of HCE and ALP in bed above their pub in Chapelizod (here they have become the Porter family), their twin sons, their daughter, and their servant. The Shem son, here called Jerry, seems to have wet the bed and cries out, bringing ALP to see to him. A mock-heroic evocation of HCE represents his stirring erection in terms of the landscape of Phoenix Park; ALP comes back to bed. The rest of the chapter gives us a series of views of HCE and ALP as they are perhaps seen by the curious twins peeping round the door. The final chapter, the only one in Book IV, begins with a series of meditations on HCE and ALP as morning comes and they, and the book, begin to wake up: 'From sleep we are passing . . . . Into the wikeawades warld from sleep we are passing' (*FW* 608. 32–4). The twenty-nine girls hail their patron saint Kevin – here, as usual, their brother Shaun – and this generates a mock biography of the saint. A dialogue between Muta and Java balances the dialogue of Mutt and Jeff in the first chapter, and the chapter concludes with another letter from ALP. This chapter of awaking and resurrection ends with dissolution and surrender of consciousness, in the marvellous deliquescing soliloquy of ALP, which mimics the flow of the river out to sea, but also, in its famous unfinished sentence, swirls us back to the opening words of the book.

The present-day reader benefits not only from the accretion of commentary and explication on the *Wake*, but also from the fact that, during the seventeen years of its composition and inter-mittent appearance, Joyce took the opportunity, both outside and inside the book, to respond to many of the expressions of bewil-derment and hostility from readers upon whose loyalty *Work in Progress*, as the book was known right up to its publication in 1939, was making intolerable demands. Ezra Pound wrote in 1926, in response to some pages that Joyce had sent him, that 'up to the present I can make nothing of it whatever. Nothing so far as I can make out, nothing short of divine vision or a new cure for the clapp can possibly be worth all the circumambient peripherization.'[1] Actually, we can see in Pound's letter the signs that, perhaps despite himself, he is beginning to make some-thing of the *Wake* – or at least that the *Wake* is beginning to make something of him. The grotesque pairing of the venerable and the venereal in Pound's objection resonates appropriately with the convergence of the divine and the profane in Joyce's own work, while Pound's own language begins to wriggle into Wakean postures; 'circumambient peripherization' is not at all bad as a bit of mimicry. (One of the few senses in which *Finnegans Wake* is actually less intimidating than *Ulysses* is in its greater imitability. There is scarcely a paragraph in *Ulysses* that I feel capable of having written; but, after a suitable period of exposure to the original, almost anyone can produce a creditable passage of Wakese.) More worrying for Joyce than the scepticism of the influential, but always prickly, Pound – who was anyway involved from the 1920s onwards in the writing of *The Cantos*, a work which made similarly extreme demands on the reader – the demands of the *Work in Progress* began to stretch the loyalty even of his patron, Harriet Shaw Weaver, upon whose generously distributed wealth Joyce and his family very largely depended for most of his later life. Joyce's brother Stanislaus, who had been a reliable supporter and advocate up to the publication of *Ulysses*, could not disguise his distaste for the 'drivelling rigmarole' which he took *Finnegans Wake* to be. It would be easy to see stubbornness or egotism in Joyce's persistence with the *Wake*, in the face of these responses.

In fact, however, there is a very large degree of interdependence between these bewildered or intolerant readings and the writing of the book. The fact that the *Wake* remained a 'work in progress' – or, to give it the name into which it warps itself in the book, a 'warping process' (*FW* 497. 3) – meant that Joyce was able to build in textual responses to these readerly reactions as he went along, cajoling, encouraging, reprimanding, instructing, and, in the process, constructing his reader. The education of particular readers which Joyce appears to have undertaken in the course of writing the book is one of the reasons that new readers of the complete text have rather more to go on than the readers of the *Work in Progress*. Indeed, one might say that the working-out of the book's self-defence, in the form of quasi-critical exegesis, comes to be a generative principle of the work itself, which distracts, protracts, but also powerfully conditions the development of the work 'itself'. A large amount of the action and dialogue in the book, for instance, is generated out of the sibling rivalry of two brothers, variously known as Shem and Shaun, Butt and Taff, Mutt and Jute, in which Joyce is in part addressing his brother Stanislaus, at once subjecting him to satirical revenge and generously giving him a voice within the text he regarded as such an unreadable waste of time. In the first chapter of Book III, which shows Shaun as the bearer of a letter written by Shem, which may therefore, like every document encountered in the *Wake*, be a miniaturization of the book itself, Shaun is allowed his own words of condemnation:

> it is not a nice production. It is a pinch of scribble, not wortha bottle of cabbis. Overdrawn! Puffedly offal tosh! Besides its auctionable, all about crime and libel! Nothing beyond clerical horrors *et omnibus* to be entered for the foreign as secondclass matter. The fuellest filth ever fired since Charley Lucan's. Flummery is what I would call it if you were to ask me to put it on a single dimension what pronounced opinion I might possibly orally have about them bagses of trash which the mother and Mr Unmentionable (O breed not his same!) has reduced to writing. (*FW* 419. 31–420.520)

Indeed, Joyce appears to have devoted a whole chapter to his work of reassurance and auto-exegesis. Chapter I.4 deals with the excavation and interpretation of an enigmatic text, the document, letter, or 'untitled mamafesta' (*FW*. 104. 4) written by ALP, which is discovered by a hen in a midden heap. Since the chapter is a simultaneous display of and discourse upon its own language and structure, it is an inviting way into the text for the new reader, whose frustration is given voice in the mock-pidgin for which Joyce had a continuing fondness: 'You is feeling like you was lost in the bush, boy? You says: It is a puling sample jungle of woods. You most shouts out: Bethicket me for a stump of a beech if I have the poultriest notion what the farest he all means' (*FW* 112. 3–6). The irony of this and many other such simulated eruptions of readerly frustration in the *Wake* is, of course, that they are given in the language against which they are permitted to protest. Indulging the protest seems doubly to undermine it. Garbled as it is by Wakean process, the protest is refused the privilege of the rationally intelligible speech on whose behalf it speaks; but, at the same time, the very intelligibility of the protest, in which, as with so much of the *Wake*, we can easily discern the syntactic shape of the sentence that is being uttered, even if we cannot account for all its lexical elements, seems to demonstrate that the *Wake* is not as unfathomable as it is being said to be.

Chapter I.4 resembles other chapters in the book in its mimicry of critical exegesis, which aims both to mock the earnestness of such commentary and to cheer it along. The commentary concerns itself with such questions as the following:

1. The authorship of the mysterious document: 'There was a time when naif alphabetters would have written it down the tracing of a purely deliquescent recidivist ... who in hallhagal write the durn thing anyhow?' (*FW* 107. 9–10, 107. 36–108. 1), suggesting that 'closer inspection of the *bordereau* would reveal a multiplicity of personalities inflicted on the document' (*FW* 107. 23–5);

2. the deleterious effects of its 'heated residence in the heart of the orangeflavoured mudmound' (*FW* 111. 33–4);

3. its eccentric lineation, with 'writing thithaways end to end and turning, turning and end to end hithaways writing and with lines of litters slittering up and louds of latters slettering down' (*FW* 114. 16–18; the associations between the processes of composting, composition, and decomposition which make up the letter here may recall Bloom's reflections on the literal composition and decomposition of letters in the 'Aeolus' chapter of *Ulysses* discussed in the last chapter);

4. the question of the 'teatimestained terminal ... a cosy little brown study all to oneself ... whether it be thumbprint, mademark or just a poor trait of the artless', the stain, whether of tea, or of urine, whether accidental or intentional (it may be a portrait of the artist, or it could be just 'a poor trait of the artless' (*FW* 114. 29–32)), which either conceals or actually is the signature to the document;

5. the perversity of the punctuation, with the 'curt witty wotty dashes never quite just right at the trim trite truth letter' (*FW* 120. 2–4);

6. the mysterious presence in the manuscript of 'numerous stabs and foliated gashes made by a pronged instrument' (*FW* 124. 2–3), explained either as scholarly vandalism, or as the indentations left by the beak of the hen who has unearthed it;

7. the sinuous intermingling of letters from different alphabets and writing systems – 'the Ostrogothic kakography

affected for certain phrases of Etruscan stabletalk . . . a constant labour to make a ghimel pass through the eye of an iota' (*FW* 120. 22–3, 26–7).

We even get a scrambled version of the letter itself, which seems no more than a chatty *mélange* of news about family, politics, and the weather, not unlike Milly Bloom's letter in *Ulysses*:

of the last of the first to Dear whom it proceeded to mention Maggy well & allathome's health well only the hate turned the mild on *the van* Houtens and the general's elections with a *lovely* face of some born gentleman with a beautiful present of wedding cakes from dear thankyou Chriesty and with grand funferall of poor Father Michael don't forget unto life's & Muggy well how are you Maggy & hopes soon to hear well & must now close it with fondest to the twoinns with four crosskisses for holy paul holey corner holipoli whollyisland pee ess from (locust may eat all but this sign shall they never) affectionate largelooking tache of tch. (*FW* 111. 10–20)

This letter reappears, with different content, but similar style, in the final chapter of the book, when it appears to have been delivered to the breakfast table of the Earwicker or Porter family. In its first appearance in chapter I.4, it is accompanied by a number of glosses, and interpretations, one apparently supplied by a Teutonic professor. (The density of the semantic overlayering in the *Wake* is often paid for by a loss of the subtly contending differences of tone and idiom of which Joyce had proved himself a master in earlier work; often, as here, the *Wake* relies on vague or crude stereotyping of voices.) The professor insists that the letter is a concealed vindication of HCE against the charges of incest and paedophilia – 'All schwants (schwrites) ischt tell the cock's trootabout him' (*FW* 113. 11–12) – and others offering psychoanalytic and Marxist readings of the letter. Pound's phrase here seems apt indeed; in the absence of the letter itself, the whole of this chapter is indeed nothing more than 'circumambient peripherization'. In a sense the whole of the *Wake* is characterized by a similar impalpability or elusiveness of the referent, a similar sense of the multiplication of interpretations of and perspectives on a series of events and characters that are never anywhere made directly available to us. The text is like a model of the expanding universe, preserving faithfully in every molecule the record of the primal explosion that brought it into being, and yet receding unstoppably away from that moment in space and time.

And yet, if the *Wake* in one sense fails to coincide with itself, there is another sense in which it cannot but thus coincide. The work of interpretation and commentary which recurs so obsessively through the text – interpretation of and by means of documents, songs, stories, riddles, rumours, and testimonies – is offered to us as a model of the work of reading the *Wake* itself. As John Paul Riquelme has suggested, this gives the *Wake* the self-implicating structure of the Moebius strip: the critical commentary on the letter here becomes the twin or mirror of the letter itself.[2] The complaint, which every reader of the *Wake* must make at some point or another, that none of the characters or events will stand still long enough to be distinguished, and that everything is tangled up with everything else, is here faithfully registered:

> every person, place and thing in the chaosmos of Alle anyway connected with the gobblydumped turkery was moving and changing every part of the time: the travelling inkhorn (possibly pot), the hare and turtle pen and paper, the continually more and less intermisunderstanding minds of the anticollaborators, the as time went on as it will variously inflected, differently pronounced, otherwise spelled, changeably meaning vocable scriptsigns. (*FW* 118. 21–8)

The text here both is and is not in the condition of which it speaks. The mutations in the language (here actually rather minimal) show us a text that is itself mobile and slippery in the manner of the text of which it speaks, in which 'chaos' and 'cosmos' will not stay at their assigned semantic distance from each other, but collapse together into 'chaosmos', and in which the mutual misunderstandings of those involved in its production (and perhaps also its interpretation) nevertheless continue to implicate the 'anticollaborators' one with another, allowing their 'intermisunderstanding' to imply not only interminable misunderstanding, but also intermittent understanding, not only interruption, but also intermingling.

Here, as elsewhere, Joyce is refusing to suppress awareness of the material conditions under which words and texts are produced and disseminated, and in referring to the 'travelling inkhorn (possibly pot)' of the mamafesta teases us with the suggestion that the letter is not in the heap of manure by accident, but perhaps also, since the inkpot may also be a teapot and a chamberpot, partakes ('kakographically', as this chapter would have it) of its excremental substance. Such an association between writing and physical waste is made elsewhere in the *Wake*, notably in the chapter devoted to a denunciation of the reprobate artist Shem, who is accused of using his own body to write with: deprived of 'romeruled stationery' in his own country, 'he winged away on a wildgoup's chase across the kathartic ocean and made synthetic ink and sensitive paper for his own end out of his wit's waste' (*FW* 185. 5–8), and produced 'nichthemerically from his unheavenly body a no uncertain quantity of obscene matter not protected by copriright in the United Stars of Ourania', writing 'over every square inch of the only foolscap available, his own body, till by its corrosive sublimation one continuous present tense integument slowly unfolded' (*FW* 185. 5–8, 29–31, 185. 35–186. 1). The principle of the recycling of waste matter extends the letter–litter associations established in *Ulysses* and also refers to the chaotic state of the materials out of which Joyce was composing the *Wake*, the voluminous notebooks and bales of paper which accompanied him on his travels around Europe, and which, on more than one occasion, risked being lost. The insistence on the physicality of the text is an acknowledgement of its vulnerability to accident and corruption. The text of *Finnegans Wake* seems to be literally, as well as semantically and stylistically, on the move.

And yet, for all the apparent insistence on the materiality of the text, and the indistinguishability of the literal and the metaphorical in the writing, the text does seem to succeed in making certain statements about itself, which may appear to exempt the narration from the general conditions which it describes and evokes. The statement that 'every person, place and thing in the chaosmos of Alle . . . was moving and changing every part of the time' actually establishes – puts in place, as we may say – a proposition which is not itself literally in motion. Paradoxically, it is at these moments of self-reflection and self-implication (literally, 'folding inwards') that *Finnegans Wake* seems to come closest to making straightforward sense. Not surprisingly, such moments are often seized upon by readers and explicators of the text (the distinction between these two functions is harder to make in the case of the *Wake* than in other works). In the very moment of acknowledging Heraclitean mutability, the book and its reader are drawn into a kind of concord, a shared and stabilizing acceptance of what Samuel Beckett smartly called 'the absolute absence of the Absolute'.[3]

Readings of the *Wake* tend not to take the full measure of this paradoxical assurance in indeterminacy, understandably, since it is hard to grasp the stabilizing and destabilizing sides of the paradox at the same time. In the course of a recent reading of the *Wake*, for example, Claudette Sartiliot uses quotations from chapter I.5 to buttress her judgement that it 'opposes all hermeneutic systems of closure (and enclosure) that rely on the supremacy of the transcendental signified (the content, the message) and thus attempt to arrest or recuperate the force or energy of the signifier'.[4] But the very demonstrability of this argument, the richness of the evidence available to confirm it in the chapter itself, cannot but begin to undermine it. How can the chapter really supply reliable statements about itself, when this is precisely the kind of content or message that is supposed to be being withheld or indefinitely disseminated? Sartiliot argues, largely on the basis of a long quotation from the chapter which parodies literary-critical discussions of the relationship between form and content, that the chapter, like the book as a whole, 'undoes the opposition between inside and outside, between *ergon* and *parergon*, between work and commentary'.[5] But, in order to borrow the authority of the text for this statement, Sartiliot is forced to reinstate the very distinction that she says is undone by the text. Jean-Michel Rabaté also examines these self-referential moments in the work, in terms of a structure of deferred and finally defeated promise; he argues that the work claims continually to offer an explication of its own mysteries, but ends up compounding them. Yet Rabaté, like Sartiliot, relies upon quotations from the text to double and as it were validate his own judgements:

> Meaning is always promised and repulsed: '(I am purposely refraining from expounding the obvious fallacy as to [. . .] the *lapses lequou* asousiated with the royal gorge)' (151. 26–9). The lapsus cuts speech short and reduces the efficacy of promise to difference of meaning. [The ellipsis here is Rabaté's own.][6]

My point here is not simply to contradict claims that *Finnegans Wake* is an unreadable, infinitely mutative, or wholly decentred or disseminative text, but rather to draw attention to the curious relationship between such claims and the authority lent to them by the text's own self-interpretations.

The question of whether *Finnegans Wake* is in fact readable in a traditional sense has helped secure for many a distinction between modernism and postmodernism. By proclaiming the power of a modernist work to trammel up every vagrant particular into its encompassing intent, *Ulysses* also offers the prospect of a totalized reading that could similarly take into account, and give an account of, every element and interconnection in the text. *Ulysses* seems to be a text that has abolished accident, comprehending it in a will-to-design so capacious (I at first wrote 'rapacious' and am not so sure that it was a mistake) that nothing could disturb its equanimity. *Finnegans Wake*, on the other hand, is nowadays almost routinely claimed as a text that is neither founded on, nor orientated towards, the possibility of a totalized or unified reading. Though he does not designate *Finnegans Wake* as postmodernist, Stephen Heath provides the terms for the distinction to be made within and beyond Joyce criticism when he writes, influentially, that 'a text such as *Finnegans Wake* is not to be read according to a process of unification. The text is not homogenous, but ceaselessly discontinuous, a hesitation of meaning into the perpetual "later"', and protests against the tendency to read 'the whole body of Joyce's work' in terms of continuity and identity.[7]

I would want to characterize *Finnegans Wake* in terms of a rather less stark choice between a modernist will-to-totality and postmodernist openness to discontinuity. *Finnegans Wake* possesses the capacity to open itself up to its outside, to every accident of reading and hermeneutic slew, while also wishing to be able to take that unaccountability into account. While most literary works come into being in the manner in which they distinguish themselves from the riotous complexity and interrupting 'noise' of social life and language, *Finnegans Wake* makes interruption a central principle. It is important not to underestimate how paradoxical this is. To say that a text is formed on and governed by the principle of interruption is to say that this principle operates continuously and, yes indeed, *uninterruptedly* through it. What is most remarkable about *Finnegans Wake* is not that it makes reading impossible, but that it makes impossible reading possible. The book is a willed suspension of the will, a designed disorder, a rational delirium, a knowing unconscious, a governed anarchy.

This leads to an interestingly indeterminate relationship between the book and its reader. On the one hand, the *Wake* outstrips any possibility of being read in the traditional sense of the term, refuses to allow even the illusion of competence; to become a skilled reader of *Finnegans Wake* is not to be initiated into a secret, but to become an expert in the manner of its mysteriousness. And yet, at the same time, as Jean-Michel Rabaté has suggested, the book exerts a more powerful claim upon its reader than perhaps any other literary work, in its urgent, repeated addresses to and invocations of the reader, and in its elaborate anticipations of his or her work:

> *Finnegans Wake* would be the total book, putting an end to the dichotomy between reader/critic and writer: 'carefully digesting the very wholesome criticism' (163. 36). Criticism is resumed, cited, consummated, and consumed in *Finnegans Wake* : it is a perpetual self-commentary which says more about itself in advance and in prolepsis than one can say about it.[8]

Jacques Derrida has also written about the rather anxious ambivalence which Joyce's work provokes. That work can be seen as a pure emptying-out, or opening onto an incalculable future, in which writing becomes a kind of gift 'before any restitution, symbolic or real . . . without return, without a sketch, even a symbolic one, of gratitude'.[9] But it can also be seen as exerting an oppressively containing force. *Finnegans Wake* in particular looks outwards to all the innumerable acts, occasions, and outcomes of its reading, but, in resigning itself to them, also seems to attempt to predict them, or keep them in mind, in a sort of prophetic archive (Derrida invents the Wakeish word 'hypermnesia' to describe it) of all possible responses to it:

> Here the event is of such plot and scope that henceforth you have only one way out: *being in memory of him*. You're not only overcome by him, whether you like it or not, but obliged by him, and constrained to measure yourself against this overcoming. Being *in memory of him*: not necessarily to remember him, no, but to be in his memory, to inhabit his memory, which is henceforth greater than all your finite memory can, in a single instant or a single vocable, gather up of culture, languages, mythologies, religions, philosophies, sciences, history of mind and of literatures.[10]

If reading Joyce involves the impossible task of trying to coincide with Joyce's memory, then that memory must be understood in more than a narrowly psychological sense. For Joyce, we can surmise, the work is not merely the mirror or precipitate of his mind and memory; it is, so to speak, its supplementary form. *Finnegans Wake* became for Joyce a machine that did his thinking and remembering for him. Not even Joyce was able to coincide with his own mind, since that mind came to be deposited in the mediated – even the mediatized – form of a work that was separate from, and excessive to, his actual subjectivity. The memory required to read *Finnegans Wake* is a supplemented memory, not just because the demands of the work are so prodigious, but also because the book is, in itself, a mnemic mechanism, a machine for anticipating and recalling itself. 'Begin to forget it,' we are counselled in the final chapter of the book. 'It will remember itself from every sides, with all gestures, in each our word' (*FW* 614. 20–1).

Finnegans Wake also responds to and is itself an effect of the more general explosion of electronic technologies for enhancing, extending, and externalizing consciousness that took place in the second phase of modern technological development. The *Wake* seems to model itself, not on the newspaper, as *Ulysses* seemed to do, but on the culture of electronic communications which was inaugurated in 1876 with the near-simultaneous invention of the telephone and the phonograph and accelerated in the early decades of the twentieth century with the rapid development of radio, cinema, and, from the mid-1920s, television. This extension of the *psyche* by and into *techne* has two distinct and separated aspects. On the one hand, the self is immeasurably enlarged; on the other, the self is thinned, scattered, decentred, objectified; the limitlessly expanded self becomes a self undefendably exposed to complexity, contradiction, and contamination. This maladjustment is noticed by Freud in his *Civilization and its Discontents* of 1930. There he celebrates the simultaneous amplification and remaking of human bodily capacities in modern technologies such as the telescope and telephone as the fulfilment of 'an ideal conception of omnipotence and omniscience', which results in man having made himself into 'a kind of prosthetic God'. Freud is more hopeful than some about the long-term prospects for technologized culture, but also notes a certain unease in technological man: 'When he puts on all his auxiliary organs he is truly magnificent; but those organs have not grown on to him and they still give him much trouble at times ... present-day man does not feel happy in his Godlike character.'[11]

Finnegans Wake expresses both the exhilaration and unease of this new expansion of being, often through the form of shifting relations between the senses, especially the two dominant senses of sight and hearing. Where *Ulysses* is still governed by the eye and by the principle of the coordination of differences and systems, *Finnegans Wake* requires and enacts the principle of aggregation which is more aptly embodied in the ear. Indeed, the conflict and cooperation of eye and ear are a recurrent motif in the *Wake*, as instanced, perhaps in this little motto from chapter III.3: 'What can't be coded can be decorded if an ear aye sieze what no eye ere grieved for' (*FW* 482. 34–6); the motto seems to advise us that what cannot be deciphered by the eye is available to be at once decoded and recorded by the more retentive and attentive ear. It was possible for Joyce to draw up a number of tables or schemas for the benefit of readers of *Ulysses*, but he never seems to have attempted anything similar for *Finnegans Wake* . Where the schema displays the completeness and finality of the work of *Ulysses*, establishing it *as* a work, or *opus*, the schema of *Finnegans Wake* is swallowed up in the metabolic workings of its self-generating self-interpretation. Perhaps the closest that Joyce came to being able to render *Finnegans Wake* in the abstract was the system of geometrical signs or 'sigla' that he generated as a shorthand way of referring to its principal characters: ⊓ was HCE, Δ was Anna Livia, [was Shem, ∧ was Shaun, and X was the collective sign for Mamalujo, the four annalist-gospellers. Interestingly, in listing these and other sigla for the benefit of Harriet Shaw Weaver early in the composition of *Finnegans Wake*, Joyce reserved one sign for the 'work in progress' itself: '□ This stands for the title but I do not wish to say it yet until the book has written more of itself' (*L*. i. 213).

Just as the mind and memory of Joyce here externalized themselves in the essentially modern – or postmodern – forms of representational apparatuses and technologies, so the *Wake* itself both borrows from and allows itself to be delivered to modern electronic media. Radio in particular features at several points in *Finnegans Wake*, both as subject and as analogy. Near the beginning of chapter II.3, there is an extended passage which seems to evoke a forthcoming inquisition of HCE in terms of the apparatus of radio transmission and reception, involving a

> tolvtubular high fidelity daildialler, as modern as tomorrow afternoon and in appearance up to the minute . . . equipped with supershielded umbrella antennas for distance-getting and connected by the magnetic links of a Bellini-Tosti coupling system with a vitaltone speaker, capable of capturing skybuddies, harbour craft emittences, key clickings, vaticum cleaners, due to woman formed mobile or man made static and bawling the whowle hamshack and wobble down in an eliminium sounds pound so as to serve him up a melegoturny marygoraumd, eclectrically filtered for allirish earths and ohmes. (*FW* 309. 14–310.1)

John Gordon sees the whole description of the 'harmonic condenser enginium' here and in the paragraph that follows as a description of the sleeping body of HCE.[12] William York Tindall suggests that this passage evokes a scene in HCE's pub, in which both HCE and his customers are engaged in the radiophonic transmission and reception of gossip and thus, presumably, collectively constitute the radiophonic apparatus.[13] One of the reasons that the chapter that follows this introduction is among the most difficult in the book is that it is itself such a densely overlaid, unpredictably interfered with, 'harmonic condenser enginium'. It is relatively easy to pick out the cadences of a police message – 'Will any persen bereaved to be passent bringback or rumpart to the Hoved politymester. Clontarf, one love, one fear' (*FW* 324. 19–21) – or a weather forecast – 'a sotten retch of low pleasure, missed in some parts but with lucal drizzles, the outlook for tomarry (Streamstress Mandig) beamed brider, his ability good' (*FW* 324. 31–4) – when these break into the stories being passed around in the pub. But it is much harder to know how we are meant to understand the long interchange between Butt and Taff telling the story of the Russian general. Are their voices supposed to be emanating from a radio in the bar? Or is the bar itself being transformed into a kind of radiophonic apparatus?

The radio returns in chapter III.3, during the long inquisition of the sleeping Yawn. Here it is only one of a number of reciprocally transforming technologies and vocal operations which operate as analogies for the scrambled communicative process in the chapter. Getting the right testimony out of Yawn, or the speakers whom the four old men attempt to summon through him, is a matter of keeping a radio set in tune, which is to say, keeping out the other voices which intrude from the ether: 'Your crackling out of your turn my Moonster firefly, like always. And 2 R.N. and Longhorns Connacht, stay off my air!' (*FW* 528. 26–8) calls out Matthew (the repulsed voices may be not only unexpected respondents but also, as William York Tindall suggests, the voices of the other three interrogators, Mark, Luke, and John, which would identify the speaker here as Matthew).[14] '2 R.N.' was the call-sign of Radio Eireann, which set up operations in 1926, '2 R.N.' being meant to evoke the phrase 'Come back to Erin'. Other technologies of vocal transmission at work in this chapter include the telephone, or 'dullaphone' (*FW* 485. 22). Later in the chapter, a telephone operator appears to break into HCE's testimony:

> – What is your numb? Bun!
> – Who gave you that numb? Poo!
> – Have you put in all your sparepennies? I'm listening. Sree!
> – Keep clear of propennies! Fore!

> (*FW* 546. 25–8)

Throughout the chapter, Joyce also develops the analogy between hearing voices on the radio and the voices summoned at a séance. The three are run together rapidly in some lines where HCE calls on his four inquisitors to verify his reputation:

> Michael Engels is your man. Let Michael relay Sutton and tell you people here who have the phoney habit (it was remarketable) in his clairaudience, as this is, as only our own Michael can, when reicherout at superstation, to bring ruptures to our roars how I am amp amp amplify. Hiemlancollin. (*FW* 533. 29–33)

Superstition is here technologized into a 'superstation', which might be an apt description of the body of Yawn, who is the medium, in both the spiritualist and the technological sense, for all the voices in this chapter. The 'clairaudience' which HCE demands is rarely provided in the chapter, however, in which confusion and 'static babel' prevail. It is not even clear whether voices are from the inside or from the outside (which implicates psychoanalytic interchange in the various interrogations undertaken in the chapter): 'I didn't say it aloud, sir', says medium Yawn in response to one question. 'I have something inside of me talking to myself' (*FW* 522. 25–6) and declares, in response to the demand 'Get yourself psychoanolised!' (*FW* 522. 31–2), 'I can psoakoonaloose myself any time I want (the fog follow you all) without your interferences' (*FW* 522. 34–5).

As in chapter II.3, radio can be seen both as a particular medium of transmission among others and as a metaphor for the dissociation, transmission, and interference of voices in general. James A. Connor usefully points to the very instability of early radio signals as a suggestive analogy for the kind of writing Joyce was undertaking in *Finnegans Wake*: 'Radio air was full of noises, wandering signals, high altitude skips, and superheterodyne screeches, and anyone who listened to it had gradually to attune himself or herself to a cacophony of voices speaking all at once.'[15] Connor presses further, to suggest, persuasively, that radio becomes a metaphor for a general interpermeability of voices, persons, and bodies which is both the condition of the *Wake* and the familiar experience of modernity:

> Not only are the dreamers connected by dream radio, but the bodies of the dreamers are themselves bound to the world. Technological consubstantiality – the mystery of radio comes home to roost. The listener, yoked to the world through his headset, writes a novel in which the characters are connected to one another, to Ireland, to the world in much the same fashion. The only difference is that this story connection is even more secure. There are no headsets, no wires that are not already parts of their bodies. Machines and flesh share functions. Thus 'man made static' is the same as 'man become static' [309. 22]. The dreamer doesn't merely listen. The dreamer is the signal, the message, and the noise. The dreamer sends and receives.[16]

The radiophonic permeability of voices in *Finnegans Wake* is the enactment of the capacity of the text to dissolve the boundary between its own inside and outside. By taking everything into itself, making of itself an infinitely capacious reservoir or receiver of voices, ideas, languages, rumours, and histories, *Finnegans Wake* also becomes a kind of transmitter, a 'radiooscillating epiepistle', as it calls itself in chapter I.5 (*FW* 108. 24), whose own signals are broadcast well beyond its own capacity to control or recall them.

In this, *Finnegans Wake* may be said to predict and exemplify the age of electronic media. Electronic media are the fulfilment of the scientific promise of universal convertibility of forces. This was discerned first of all in the thermodynamic era which extended from the late eighteenth century to the late nineteenth century (which we may identify broadly with Lewis Mumford's age of 'palaeotechnics'). In this era, the emphasis fell upon the derivation of physical work from thermodynamic conversion, in which technology acts principally as the augmentation of raw muscle power. This is succeeded, with the invention of the telegraph and, later in the century, of the telephone and the phonograph in 1876 and 1877, and then by the development of broadcast media such as radio, cinema, and TV, by the age of electromagnetic conversion, which is broadly coincident with Mumford's age of 'neotechnics'.[17] Now the emphasis falls upon the prosthetic enhancement of the senses, especially the senses of hearing and sight. The outcomes of this kind of technology are not so easily measurable in terms of amounts of work performed. It is followed from the end of the Second World War by our own digital age, which is characterized by universal convertibility. Now, every conceivable form of input may be rendered in terms of information and transformed into any desirable output. In this dispensation, value no longer resides in the quantitative gain of output achieved as a result of the conversion of heat into motive power, for example, or acoustic stimulus into electronic signal. Rather, value is derived from the speed or multiplicity of conversions themselves. If *Ulysses* can be seen as a verbal technology in which a mass of initially unintegrated particulars, or noise, is rendered systematic, thus producing the greatest imaginable informational yield, then *Finnegans Wake* appears as a different kind of technology, a technology in which the intensity of transformations and translations is the central principle. Thus, where *Ulysses* aims to coordinate the senses one with another, and to coordinate systems into correspondences – the physiological system of the body and the rhetorical system of language, for example – what matters in *Finnegans Wake* appears to be the speed of the mutative interactions of the different senses, especially those of sight and hearing. A little earlier, I read the phrase 'What can't be coded can be decorded if an ear aye sieze what no eye ere grieved for' (FW 482. 34–6), as a celebration of the advantage of the ear over the eye, but its manner obviously invites us, as the *Wake* does as a whole, to experience their cooperation; the advantage of the ear may lie precisely in its deficiency, its tendency to associate with other senses. Technology in the contemporary world is best thought of, not in terms of the process of extracting work, but in terms of translations; if this linguistic metaphor seems to suggest a master-code, a universal grammar of translation, then it is also the case that language itself is subject in the digital age to translation into other systems. The principle of translation is anticipated in what I have called the thermodynamic and electromagnetic eras too, for there is an interesting correspondence between the linguistic forms in which technology impacted on public awareness, which is to say through the explosion of words such as 'telephone', 'phonograph', 'gramophone', 'television', and even 'thermodynamic' and 'electromagnetic' themselves, as well as less well-known agglomerations like 'phonautograph', 'photophone', and 'magnetophone'. All of these new words anticipate the coinages, convergences, and lexical miscegenations of *Finnegans Wake*, which famously calls itself a 'collideorscape' (*FW* 143. 28), in the manner in which they signal the conversion of different physical systems one into another. I can remember being taught in school by a disapproving etymological purist that the word 'television' was an unacceptable mongrel (despite being universally accepted of course), because it ran together words derived from Greek and Latin. The collapse of distinctions enacted in the word nicely mimics the conversion of physical systems one into another upon which so much modern technology depends and the collapse of cultural distinctions which such technology appears to portend.

Perhaps the best evidence of *Finnegans Wake* 's affinity to the digital age is the fact that it is itself so resistant to translation. The difficulty of translating *Finnegans Wake* comes partly from the difficulty of deciding what language it is in the first place at any particular moment. But the fact that translations are not only repeatedly attempted, but also keep being shown to be in part possible, is perhaps a proof of how close *Finnegans Wake* is to an age of universal cultural encroachment, in which no single language can be sheltered from interruption by other voices, other languages, other histories. *Finnegans Wake* both belongs to this culture of interruptions and enacts a kind of technological process upon it, in the way in which it, so to speak, translates interruption into translation; every interruption, or intrusion of the alien or the irrelevant, is turned into a connection or association.

It is perhaps not surprising then that the increasing interest in applying contemporary computer technology to the study and reading of Joyce should begin to disclose a profound affinity between such technologies and their object. If *Ulysses* and *Finnegans Wake* call for the resources of hypertext and multi-media databases to make visible and available the wealth of interconnections of which each consists, then this is perhaps partly because the works themselves appear singly or collectively to be what Derrida, again spurred into Wakean imitation, has called a 'programotelephonic encyclopaedia'.[18] Even more extravagantly, perhaps, though in a hyperbolic mode that is in oddly exact congruence with that of the text he is discussing, Derrida describes Joyce's work as

> this 1000th generation computer – *Ulysses, Finnegans Wake* – besides which the current technology of our computers and our micro-computerified archives and our translating machines remains a *bricolage* of a prehistoric child's toys. And above all its mechanisms are of a slowness incommensurable with the quasi-infinite speed of the movements on Joyce's cables. How could you calculate the speed with which a mark, a marked piece of information, is placed in contact with another in the same word or from one end of the book to another?[19]

Derrida concludes that, even were one able to construct a technology capable of making the multiple connections that are made in the reading of *Finnegans Wake*, or the relaying process by which it, as it were, reads itself through the readings conducted of it, this could succeed only in mimicking what Joyce has already achieved, and would be thus no more than 'the double or the simulation of the event "Joyce", the name of Joyce, the signed work, the Joyce software today, joyceware'.[20]

In a curious way, *Finnegans Wake* may begin to be naturalized through contemporary developments in information technology, as they habituate us to the idea of a technological sublime, or a soft infinity of links, analogies, and mutations. Similarly, a world in which work will be concentrated around and identified with the production and deployment of certain kinds of information rather than the production and consumption of concrete goods may be a world that is more at ease with the interminability of *Finnegans Wake* and the work of its reading. I suggested in my first chapter that the heroic ideal of the work of art in modernism was both a mimicry and a transfiguring refusal of the new identification between work and the individual subject that arose during the nineteenth century. It may be that *Finnegans Wake* (and perhaps Joyce's work as a whole, to the degree that the experience of reading the *Wake* begins to transform our understanding of that work, along with our understanding of the ideas of work and wholeness as such) has the same relation of mimicry and refusal to the changing relations between work and selfhood in the twentieth century. The movement of Joyce's work, as it has been followed through in this book, suggests the gradual dissolution of the defining relationship between the artist and his work, a work that is both self-sufficient and yet also the image and guarantee of the unique and originating power of the artist. *Finnegans Wake* may appear to anticipate a world in which, to borrow the words of Cassio in Shakespeare's *Othello*, our occupation's gone; a world in which the defining link between an individual's work and his or her subjecthood is on the point of vanishing. The text which was known for so long as *Work in Progress* that the actual title arrived as a kind of subtitle or afterthought is the immensely laborious manufacture of a different kind of work, which offers no such confirming mirror of the originating self's powers of self-origination. Rather than a work, in the traditional sense, the text is a set of procedures, processes, and workings.

It is not that the text has become any less unreadable; rather it may be that the transformed and transforming experiences of information technology may have begun to modify the meaning of that unreadability, diminishing its demands upon us, and blunting its provocation. The very capacity to conceive of the '1000th generation computer', which Derrida flourishes as a way of asserting the sublime unencompassability of the *Wake* and Joyce's work in general, suggests in fact that the *Wake* may be in danger of being both outstripped and put in its place by our routine evocation of the technological sublime.

Under these circumstances, we would do well perhaps to reconsider the question of the work of reading the *Wake*. When the provocations of unreadability and immeasurable complexity have become such a matter of routine, might there not be a greater challenge in the idea that *Finnegans Wake* can offer us a kind of fix upon unencompassability, a means of orientating ourselves to that world of constructed connections and correspondences with which we can never hope to coincide? *Finnegans Wake* would then prefigure, not a mere surrender to the soft infinity of contemporary technological culture, but, borrowing Freud's term, a form of cultural 'dreamwork' which can make it possible to represent to ourselves our relation and response to the unrepresentable, as well as our continuing responsibility to it.

Notes

Chapter 1. Introduction: The Workings of Work

1. Stanislaus Joyce, *My Brother's Keeper*, ed. Richard Ellmann (London: Faber & Faber, 1958), 166.
2. Michel Foucault, `What Is An Author?', in *Textual Strategies*, ed. Josué V. Harari (London: Methuen, 1979), 154.
3. Samuel Beckett, 'Three Dialogues With Georges Duthuit', in *Disjecta: Miscellaneous Writings and a Dramatic Fragment*, ed. Ruby Cohn (London: John Calder, 1983), 145. I have discussed the two alternative economies of artistic value at greater length in my *Theory and Cultural Value* (Oxford: Blackwell, 1992), 57–101.

Chapter 2. The Indefinite Article: *Dubliners*

1. Richard Pearce, *The Politics of Narration: James Joyce, William Faulkner, and Virginia Woolf* (New Brunswick: Rutgers University Press, 1991), 27–36.
2. Ibid. 27.
3. Oliver St John Gogarty, *As I Was Going Down Sackville Street* (New York: Harvest, 1967), 294–5.
4. Stanislaus Joyce, unpublished notes on Joyce, quoted in Richard Ellmann, *James Joyce* (2nd edn., Oxford: Oxford University Press, 1982), 163.

Chapter 3. Workshop and Labyrinth: *A Portrait of the Artist as a Young Man*

1. *The Letters of John Keats 1814–21*, ed. Hyder H. Rollins (2 vols; Cambridge, Mass.: Harvard University Press, 1958), ii. 102.

2. Nancy Chodorow, *The Reproduction of Mothering: Psycho-analysis and the Sociology of Gender* (Berkeley and Los Angeles: University of California Press, 1978).
3. Hugh Kenner, *Joyce's Voices* (Berkeley and Los Angeles: University of California Press, 1978), 17.
4. Letter from Joyce's secretary to Theodore Spencer, quoted in *SH* 11–12.
5. The struggle between Stephen's voices and the voices of cultural authority is well described by Marguerite Harkness, in *A Portrait of the Artist as a Young Man: Voices of the Text* (Boston: Twayne, 1990), esp. 21–36.

CHAPTER 4. 'LITERATURE &': *ULYSSES*

1. One of the most emphatic arguments for reading Ulysses as a series of encounters between the contrary principles represented by Stephen and Bloom is Richard Ellmann's *Ulysses on the Liffey* (London: Faber & Faber, 1972). The fullest exploration of the theme of the relationship between artistic and civic identity in the book is to be found in Charles Peake, *James Joyce: The Citizen and the Artist* (London: Edward Arnold, 1977).
2. Sheldon Brivic, *The Veil of Signs: Joyce, Lacan, and Perception* (Urbana, Ill.: University of Illinois Press, 1991), 9.
3. Stanislaus Joyce, *My Brother's Keeper,* ed. Richard Ellmann (London: Faber & Faber, 1958), 105–6.
4. Frank Budgen, *James Joyce and the Making of 'Ulysses'* (London: Grayson & Grayson, 1937), 21.
5. Ibid.
6. See Michael Groden (ed.), *The James Joyce Archives,* xxiii. *Ulysses: 'Aeolus', 'Lestrygonians', 'Scylla and Charybdis' and 'Wandering Rocks': A Facsimile of Placards for Episodes 7–10* (New York: Garland Publishing 1978) 13–20.
7. See Don Gifford and Robert J. Seidman, *Ulysses Annotated: Notes for James Joyce's 'Ulysses'* (2nd edn., Berkeley and Los Angeles: University of California Press, 1989), 150.
8. Budgen, *James Joyce and the Making of 'Ulysses',* 234.
9. Stuart Gilbert, *James Joyce's 'Ulysses': A Study* (1930; rev. edn., London: Faber & Faber, 1952).

10. Many of these negative responses are gathered together in Marvin Magalaner and Richard M. Kain, *James Joyce: The Man, The Work, the Reputation* (New York: New York University Press, 1956), 163–215, and Robert H. Deming (ed.), *James Joyce: The Critical Heritage* (2 vols.; London: Routledge & Kegan Paul, 1970), i. 184–370.

11. Wyndham Lewis, *Time and Western Man* (London: Chatto & Windus, 1927).

12. Among the most important and influential texts in the assimilation of Joyce to modernism are Harry Levin, *James Joyce: A Critical Introduction* (New York: New Directions, 1941), Hugh Kenner, *Dublin's Joyce* (London: Chatto & Windus, 1956), and S. L. Goldberg, *The Classical Temper: A Study of James Joyce's 'Ulysses'* (London: Chatto & Windus, 1961).

CHAPTER 5. A *WAKE* IN PROGRESS: *FINNEGANS WAKE*

1. *The Letters of Ezra Pound 1907–1941*, ed. D. D. Paige (London: Faber & Faber, 1951), 202.

2. John Paul Riquelme, *Teller and Tale in Joyce's Fiction: Oscillating Perspectives* (Baltimore: Johns Hopkins University Press, 1983), 11–14, 25–8.

3. Samuel Beckett, 'Dante...Bruno.Vico..Joyce', in Samuel Beckett *et al.*, *Our Exagmination Round His Factification for Incamination of Work in Progress* (1929; London: Faber & Faber, 1972), 22.

4. Claudette Sartiliot, *Citation and Modernity: Derrida, Joyce, and Brecht* (Norman and London: University of Nebraska Press, 1994), 105.

5. Ibid. 104.

6. Jean-Michel Rabaté, 'Lapsus Ex Machina', trans. Elizabeth Guild, in Derek Attridge and Daniel Ferrer (eds.), *Post-Structuralist Joyce: Essays from the French*, (Cambridge: Cambridge University Press, 1984), 93.

7. Stephen Heath, 'Ambiviolences: Notes For Reading Joyce', trans. Isabelle Mahieu, in ibid. 32–3.

8. Rabaté, 'Lapsus Ex Machina', in ibid. 98.

9. Jacques Derrida, 'Two Words for Joyce', trans. Geoffrey Bennington, in ibid. 146.

10. Ibid. 147.

11. Freud, *Civilization and its Discontents,* in *Civilization, Society and Religion* (Pelican Freud Library, 12; Harmondsworth: Penguin, 1985), 280.
12. John Gordon, *'Finnegans Wake': A Plot Summary* (Dublin: Gill & Macmillan, 1986), 194–5.
13. William York Tindall, *A Reader's Guide to 'Finnegans Wake'* (London: Thames & Hudson, 1969), 189.
14. Ibid. 270.
15. James A. Connor, 'Radio Free Joyce: *Wake* Language and the Experience of Radio', *James Joyce Quarterly,* 30–1 (1993), 826.
16. Ibid. 831–2.
17. Lewis Mumford, *Technics and Civilization* (New York: Harcourt Brace, 1934), 212–67.
18. Jacques Derrida, 'Ulysses Gramophone: Hear Say Yes in Joyce', trans. Tina Kendall and Shari Benstock, in Jacques Derrida, ed. Derek Attridge, *Acts of Literature* (London: Routledge, 1992), 283.
19. Derrida, 'Two Words for Joyce', 147.
20. Ibid. 148. The analogies between Joyce's work and the structure of contemporary cyberspace have been discussed in detail by Donald Theall, in his 'Beyond the Orality/Literacy Dichotomy: James Joyce and the Prehistory of Cyberspace', *Postmodern Culture,* 2/3 (1992). *Postmodern Culture* is an electronic journal, and this article is accessible at the URL: http://jefferson.village.virginia.edu/pmc/issue.592/theall.592.

Select Bibliography

EDITIONS

The situation with regard to editions of Joyce's works is complex. In 1989, Joyce's works came out of copyright in the UK and the USA. New editions of many of Joyce's works appeared shortly after this date, many of which are still available, despite the fact that, as a result of a change in European Community copyright law, Joyce's works have now gone back into copyright in Europe. Because of the number of competing texts currently available, I have decided in this book to use the scholarly critical editions of *Dubliners* and *A Portrait of the Artist as a Young Man* issued by Garland Press, and the Penguin Student's Edition of *Ulysses*, which is set from the Garland Press edition, as indicated in the Abbreviations, above. Arguments for and against the Garland Press *Ulysses* are still being produced, but the text has established itself as a standard one for Joyce criticism because its numbered lines allow pinpointing of references. Details are given below of editions of other Joyce works, and other editions of the principal works which are of particular interest.

The Critical Writings of James Joyce, ed. Richard Ellmann and Ellsworth Mason (London: Faber & Faber, 1959).

Dubliners (London: Jonathan Cape, 1967). This edition was standard until it was recently superseded by the Garland Press edition used for this book.

Poems and Exiles, ed. J. C. C. Mays (Harmondsworth: Penguin, 1992). All of Joyce's poetry is made available in this edition, along with his only play.

A Portrait of the Artist as a Young Man, ed. Chester Anderson and Richard Ellmann (New York: Viking Press, 1964). This edition was supplemented by *A Portrait of the Artist as a Young Man*, ed. R. B. Kershner (Boston: Bedford Books/St Martin's Press, 1993), which also supplies historical and critical contexts for the novel. Both of these have now been superseded by the Garland Press edition used for this book.

103

Ulysses, ed. Jeri Johnson (Oxford: Oxford University Press, 1992). This reprints the text of the first edition of the novel published in 1922.

Ulysses: A Critical and Synoptic Edition, ed. Hans Walter Gabler with Wolfhard Steppe and Claus Melchior (3 vols.; New York: Garland, 1984). The lineation and line-numbering used in this text are reproduced in the Bodley Head and Penguin Student's Edition.

Ulysses: The Corrected Text, ed. Hans Walter Gabler with Wolfhard Steppe and Claus Melchior (London: Bodley Head, 1986). This reproduces the lineation and line-numbering of the 1984 Garland edition, and is identical in pagination, lineation, and line-numbering to the Penguin Student's Edition.

Groden, Michael (ed.), *The James Joyce Archives* (63 vols.; New York: Garland Publishing, 1977–8). A facsimile edition of much of the manuscript and other material relating to the composition of Joyce's works.

BIOGRAPHY

Ellmann, Richard, *James Joyce* (2nd edn., London: Oxford University Press, 1982). A monumental biography, which, like Joyce's own work, is encrusted with fascinating details, but sometimes a little lacking in plot impetus.

Joyce, Stanislaus, *My Brother's Keeper*, (ed.) Richard Ellmann (London: Faber & Faber, 1958). Partisan, sometimes dubious in its judgements, but a fascinating insight into Joyce's life as seen by his brother.

CRITICAL STUDIES

Attridge, Derek, and Ferrer, Daniel (eds.), *Post-Structuralist Joyce: Essays from the French* (Cambridge: Cambridge University Press, 1984). An influential collection of essays showing the remarkable impact of Joyce studies on French poststructuralism and vice versa.

Brivic, Sheldon, *The Veil of Signs: Joyce, Lacan, and Perception* (Urbana, Ill.: University of Illinois Press, 1991). A psychoanalytic reading of Joyce which draws on the work of Jacques Lacan.

Brown, Richard, *James Joyce: A Post-Culturalist Perspective* (Basingstoke: Macmillan, 1992). A sparky, economical, and up to date general introduction to Joyce..

Burgess, Anthony, *Here Comes Everybody: An Introduction to James Joyce for the Ordinary Reader* (London: Faber & Faber, 1965). A vigorous and enthusiastic way in to Joyce's writing.

Cheng, Vincent J., *Joyce, Race, and Empire* (Cambridge: Cambridge University Press, 1995). An illuminating account of Joyce from the perspective of postcolonial theory.

Deming, Robert H. (ed.), *James Joyce: The Critical Heritage* (2 vols.; London: Routledge & Kegan Paul, 1970). A very useful collection of early critical responses to Joyce's works.

Derrida, Jacques, 'Ulysses Gramophone: Hear Say Yes in Joyce', trans. Tina Kendall and Shari Benstock, in Jacques Derrida ed. Derek Attridge, *Acts of Literature*, (London: Routledge, 1992), 253–309. An extraordinary, free-ranging speculation about telephones, gramophones, and the mobility of the word 'yes' in *Ulysses*.

Goldberg, S. L., *The Classical Temper: A Study of James Joyce's 'Ulysses'* (London: Chatto & Windus, 1961). Still one of the best introductions to Joyce's aesthetic theory.

Henke, Suzette, *James Joyce and the Politics of Desire* (London: Routledge, 1990). A feminist-psychoanalytic perspective on Joyce.

Herr, Cheryl, *Joyce's Anatomy of Culture* (Urbana, Ill.: University of Illinois Press, 1986). An absorbing, and much-needed study of the contexts for Joyce's work in early twentieth-century Irish cultural history.

Kenner, Hugh, *Joyce's Voices* (Berkeley and Los Angeles: University of California Press, 1978). An excellent discussion of the question of voice and narrative authority in Joyce's work.

MacCabe, Colin, *James Joyce and the Revolution of the Word* (Basingstoke: Macmillan, 1979). The influential first poststructuralist reading of Joyce to appear in English.

Magalaner, Marvin, and Kain, Richard M., *James Joyce: The Man, The Work, the Reputation* (New York: New York University Press, 1956). A somewhat shaky general critical guide, but it does include some excellent discussions of the reception of Joyce's work, especially *Ulysses*.

Mahaffey, Vikki, *Re-authorizing Joyce* (Cambridge: Cambridge University Press, 1986). Argues engagingly that Joyce's writing reworks the idea and nature of cultural authority.

Manganiello, Dominic, *Joyce's Politics* (London: Routledge & Kegan Paul, 1980). A wide-ranging and informative study of the political contexts for Joyce's writing, a somewhat neglected topic up to this point in Joyce criticism.

Parrinder, Patrick, *James Joyce* (Cambridge: Cambridge University Press, 1984). A generous, intelligent overview of Joyce.

Rabaté, Jean-Michel, *James Joyce: Authorized Reader* (Baltimore: Johns Hopkins University Press, 1991). A dazzling, demanding work by one of the most brilliant and provocative of contemporary poststructuralist commentators on the work of Joyce.

Roughley, Alan, *James Joyce and Critical Theory: An Introduction* (Hemel Hempstead: Harvester/Wheatsheaf, 1991). Discusses a range of different contemporary critical approaches as they have been directed at the work of Joyce.

Scott, Bonnie Kime, *Joyce and Feminism* (Bloomington, Ind.: Indiana University Press, 1984). One of the earliest attempts to reconsider Joyce's work in the light of feminist theory.

Dubliners

Torchiana, Donald, *Backgrounds for Joyce's Dubliners* (London: Allen & Unwin, 1986).

A Portrait of the Artist as a Young Man

Connolly, Thomas (ed.), *Joyce's Portrait: Criticisms and Critiques* (London: Owen, 1962). Includes a number of important and influential readings of the *Portrait* in modernist terms.

Gifford, Don, *Joyce Annotated: Notes for Dubliners and a Portrait of the Artist as a Young Man* (Berkeley and Los Angeles: University of California Press, 1982).

Harkness, Marguerite, *A Portrait of the Artist as a Young Man: Voices of the Text* (Boston: Twayne, 1990). A clear and accessible account of the novel, which focuses on the struggle between Stephen and the authoritative voices of culture.

Thornton, Weldon, *The Antimodernism of Joyce's Portrait of the Artist as a Young Man* (Syracuse, NY: Syracuse University Press, 1994). A provocative, well-sustained argument for the *Portrait* as a text which prefigures postmodernism.

Ulysses

Blamires, Harry, *The New Bloomsday Book* (London: Routledge, 1988). One of the best beginner's guides, which takes the reader through the novel chapter by chapter with sensible and helpful explications.

Budgen, Frank, *James Joyce and the Making of 'Ulysses'* (London: Grayson & Grayson, 1937). A book written by one of Joyce's closest friends and confidants during the writing of *Ulysses*, that gives intriguing and illuminating reports on Joyce's attitudes and intentions in writing the book.

Ellmann, Richard, *Ulysses on the Liffey* (London: Faber and Faber, 1972). A classic study, which centres around the conflict of body and soul and its resolution.

French, Marilyn, *The Book as World: James Joyce's 'Ulysses'* (Cambridge, Mass.: Harvard University Press, 1976). A vigorous, humane, and accessibly written study of the relations between the competing demands of the world and the book in Joyce's work.

Gifford Don, and Seidman, Robert J., *Ulysses Annotated: Notes for James Joyce's 'Ulysses'* (2nd edn., Berkeley and Los Angeles: University of

California Press, 1989). An indispensable reference work. While it does not answer every question about *Ulysses*, it answers more than any other equivalent volume.

Gilbert, Stuart, *James Joyce's Ulysses: A Study* (1930; rev. edn., London: Faber & Faber, 1952). The first full-length study of Joyce's *Ulysses*, for which Gilbert drew on his friendship with Joyce. A classic text which is still full of interest.

Groden, Michael, *Ulysses in Progress* (Princeton: Princeton University Press, 1980). An account of the complex evolution of the book through its different manuscript and publishing stages.

Hart, Clive, and Hayman, David (eds.), *Ulysses: Critical Essays* (Berkeley and Los Angeles: University of California Press, 1974). This provides a substantial essay on each episode of the book, and is still one of the most useful collections about *Ulysses*.

Herring, Philip, *Joyce's Notes and Early Drafts for 'Ulysses'* (Charlottesville, Va.: University Press of Virginia, 1977). Especially informative about the revisions to the later episodes of the book.

Lawrence, Karen, *The Odyssey of Style in Joyce's 'Ulysses'* (Princeton: Princeton University Press, 1981). A clear and thoughtful analysis of the shifts of style from chapter to chapter of *Ulysses*.

Finnegans Wake

Beckett, Samuel, *et al.*, *Our Exagmination Round His Factification for Incamination of Work in Progress* (1929; London: Faber & Faber, 1972). A volume of early responses to *Finnegans Wake*, partly sponsored by Joyce. The essay by Beckett himself, 'Dante. . .Bruno.Vico. .Joyce', is of particular interest.

Benstock, Bernard, *Joyce-Again's Wake: An Analysis of 'Finnegans Wake'* (Seattle: Washington University Press, 1965). Organized as a thematic analysis, but does include a handy summary of events in each chapter of the *Wake*.

Campbell Joseph, and Robinson, Henry Morton, *A Skeleton Key to Finnegans Wake* (London: Faber & Faber, 1947). Bits of the key have got a little stiff and rusty with the passing of years, but, as a clear, continuous account of the *Wake*, it still has much to recommend it.

Gordon, John, *'Finnegans Wake': A Plot Summary* (Dublin: Gill & Macmillan, 1986). A continuous, chapter-by-chapter explication, which often departs from accepted readings of the 'narrative' of *Finnegans Wake* in surprising and suggestive ways.

Hart, Clive, *Structure and Motif in Finnegans Wake* (London: Faber, 1962). An informative study of recurrent motifs and syntactical patterns in the text.

Hayman, David, *A First-Draft Version of Finnegans Wake* (Berkeley and Los Angeles: University of California Press, 1963). A very helpful resource, both for the novice reader and the reader with an interest in the composition history of the *Wake*.

Hayman, David, *The 'Wake' in Transit* (Ithaca, NY: Cornell University Press, 1991). An excellent, detailed study of the complicated story of the evolution of the *Wake*, which nevertheless leaves much in this area still to be done.

Hofheinz, Thomas C., *Joyce and the Invention of Irish History: Finnegans Wake in Context* (Cambridge: Cambridge University Press, 1995). An excellent consideration both of historical themes and the treatment of the problem of history as such in the *Wake*.

McHugh, Roland, *Annotations to Finnegans Wake* (London: Routledge, 1980). An impressive gathering-together of glosses of the text, handily displayed in a format that mirrors the pagination and lineation of the Faber editions, in a cross between a medieval interlineated gloss and the hypertext databases of the *Wake*-explications currently under development. Though it often leaves substantial stretches of text unexplicated, it is the basis for all close readings.

Rose, Danis, and O'Hanlon, John, *Understanding Finnegans Wake* (New York: Garland, 1982). A fluent, continuous, chapter-by-chapter explication.

Tindall, William York, *A Reader's Guide to 'Finnegans Wake'* (London: Thames & Hudson, 1969). A chapter-by-chapter explication, bittier than some others, but often sharply illuminating too.

Index

*Recent and
Forthcoming Titles
in the
New Series of*

WRITERS AND
THEIR WORK

---

*"...this series promises to outshine its own
previously high reputation."*
Times Higher Education Supplement

*"...will build into a fine multi-volume critical
encyclopaedia of English literature."*
Library Review & Reference Review

"...Excellent, informative, readable, and recommended."
NATE News

"...promises to be a rare series of creative scholarship."
Times Educational Supplement

WRITERS AND THEIR WORK

RECENT & FORTHCOMING TITLES

Title	Author
W.H. Auden	*Stan Smith*
Aphra Behn	*Sue Wiseman*
Lord Byron	*J. Drummond Bone*
Angela Carter	*Lorna Sage*
Geoffrey Chaucer	*Steve Ellis*
Children's Literature	*Kimberley Reynolds*
John Clare	*John Lucas*
Joseph Conrad	*Cedric Watts*
John Donne	*Stevie Davies*
Henry Fielding	*Jenny Uglow*
Elizabeth Gaskell	*Kate Flint*
William Golding	*Kevin McCarron*
Graham Greene	*Peter Mudford*
Hamlet	*Ann Thompson & Neil Taylor*
Thomas Hardy	*Peter Widdowson*
David Hare	*Jeremy Ridgman*
Tony Harrison	*Joe Kelleher*
William Hazlitt	*J.B. Priestley; R.L. Brett (introduction by Michael Foot)*
Seamus Heaney	*Andrew Murphy*
George Herbert	*T.S. Eliot (introduction by Peter Porter)*
Henry James - The Later Writing	*Barbara Hardy*
James Joyce	*Steven Connor*
King Lear	*Terence Hawkes*
Doris Lessing	*Elizabeth Maslen*
David Lodge	*Bernard Bergonzi*
Christopher Marlowe	*Thomas Healy*
Andrew Marvell	*Annabel Patterson*
Ian McEwan	*Kiernan Ryan*
A Midsummer Night's Dream	*Helen Hackett*
Walter Pater	*Laurel Brake*
Jean Rhys	*Helen Carr*
Dorothy Richardson	*Carol Watts*
The Sensation Novel	*Lyn Pykett*
Edmund Spenser	*Colin Burrow*
J.R.R. Tolkien	*Charles Moseley*
Leo Tolstoy	*John Bayley*
Virginia Woolf	*Laura Marcus*
Charlotte Yonge	*Alethea Hayter*

TITLES IN PREPARATION

Title	Author
Peter Ackroyd	*Susana Onega*
Antony and Cleopatra	*Ken Parker*
Jane Austen	*Robert Clark*
Samuel Beckett	*Keir Elam*
William Blake	*John Beer*
Elizabeth Bowen	*Maud Ellmann*
Emily Brontë	*Stevie Davies*
A.S. Byatt	*Richard Todd*
Caryl Churchill	*Elaine Aston*
S.T. Coleridge	*Stephen Bygrave*
Crime Fiction	*Martin Priestman*
Charles Dickens	*Rod Mengham*
Carol Ann Duffy	*Deryn Rees Jones*
Daniel Defoe	*Jim Rigney*
George Eliot	*Josephine McDonagh*
E.M. Forster	*Nicholas Royle*
Brian Friel	*Geraldine Higgins*
Henry IV	*Peter Bogdanov*
Henrik Ibsen	*Sally Ledger*
Rudyard Kipling	*Jan Montefiore*
Franz Kafka	*Michael Wood*
John Keats	*Kelvin Everest*
Philip Larkin	*Laurence Lerner*
D.H. Lawrence	*Linda Ruth Williams*
Measure for Measure	*Kate Chedgzoy*
William Morris	*Anne Janowitz*
Brian Patten	*Linda Cookson*
Alexander Pope	*Pat Rogers*
Sylvia Plath	*Elizabeth Bronfen*
Richard II	*Margaret Healy*
Lord Rochester	*Peter Porter*
Romeo and Juliet	*Sasha Roberts*
Christina Rossetti	*Kathryn Burlinson*
Salman Rushdie	*Damian Grant*
Sir Walter Scott	*John Sutherland*
Stevie Smith	*Alison Light*
Wole Soyinka	*Mpalive Msiska*
Laurence Sterne	*Manfred Pfister*
Jonathan Swift	*Claude Rawson*
The Tempest	*Gordon McMullan*
Mary Wollstonecraft	*Jane Moore*
Evelyn Waugh	*Malcolm Bradbury*
John Webster	*Thomas Sorge*
Angus Wilson	*Peter Conradi*
William Wordsworth	*Nicholas Roe*
Working Class Fiction	*Ian Haywood*
W.B. Yeats	*Ed Larrissy*

PUBLISHED

DORIS LESSING
Elizabeth Maslen

Covering a wide range of Doris Lessing's works up to 1992, including all
her novels and a selection of her short stories and non-fictional writing,
this study demonstrates how Lessing's commitment to political and
cultural issues and her explorations of inner space have remained
unchanged throughout her career. Maslen also examines Lessing's
writings in the context of the work of Bakhtin and Foucault, and of
feminist theories.

Elizabeth Maslen is Senior Lecturer in English at Queen Mary and
Westfield College, University of London.

0 7463 0705 5 paperback 80pp £5.99

JOSEPH CONRAD
Cedric Watts

This authoritative introduction to the range of Conrad's work draws out
the distinctive thematic preoccupations and technical devices running
through the main phases of the novelist's literary career. Watts explores
Conrad's importance and influence as a moral, social and political
commentator on his times and addresses recent controversial
developments in the evaluation of this magisterial, vivid, complex and
problematic author.

Cedric Watts, Professor of English at the University of Sussex, is
recognized internationally as a leading authority on the life and works of
Joseph Conrad.

0 7463 0737 3 paperback 80pp £5.99

JOHN DONNE
Stevie Davies

Raising a feminist challenge to the body of male criticism which
congratulates Donne on the 'virility' of his writing, Dr Davies' stimulating
and accessible introduction to the full range of the poet's work sets it in
the wider cultural, religious and political context conditioning the mind of
this turbulent and brilliant poet. Davies also explores the profound
emotionalism of Donne's verse and offers close, sensitive readings of
individual poems.

Stevie Davies is a literary critic and novelist who has written on a wide
range of literature.

0 7463 0738 1 paperback 96pp £6.99

IAN McEWAN
Kiernan Ryan

This is the first book-length study of one of the most original and exciting writers to have emerged in Britain in recent years. It provides an introduction to the whole range of McEwan's work, examining his novels, short stories and screenplays in depth and tracing his development from the 'succès de scandale' of *First Love, Last Rites* to the haunting vision of the acclaimed *Black Dogs*.

Kiernan Ryan is Fellow and Director of Studies in English at New Hall, University of Cambridge.

0 7463 0742 X paperback c96pp £6.99

ELIZABETH GASKELL
Kate Flint

Recent critical appraisal has focused on Gaskell both as a novelist of industrial England and on her awareness of the position of women and the problems of the woman writer. Kate Flint reveals how for Gaskell the condition of women was inseparable from broader issues of social change. She shows how recent modes of feminist criticism and theories of narrative work together to illuminate the radicalism and experimentalism which we find in Gaskell's fiction.

Kate Flint is University Lecturer in Victorian and Modern English Literature, and Fellow of Linacre College, Oxford.

0 7463 0718 7 paperback 96pp c£5.99

KING LEAR
Terence Hawkes

In his concise but thorough analysis of *King Lear* Terence Hawkes offers a full and clear exposition of its complex narrative and thematic structure. By examining the play's central preoccupations and through close analysis of the texture of its verse he seeks to locate it firmly in its own history and the social context to which, clearly, it aims to speak. The result is a challenging critical work which both deepens understanding of this great play and illuminates recent approaches to it.

Terence Hawkes has written several books on both Shakespeare and modern critical theory. he is Professor of English at the University of Wales, Cardiff.

0 7463 0739 X paperback 96pp c£5.99

THE SENSATION NOVEL
Lyn Pykett

A 'great fact' in the literature of its day, a 'disagreeable' sign of the times, or an ephemeral minor sub-genre? What was the sensation novel, and why did it briefly dominate the literary scene in the 1860s? This wide-ranging study analyses the broader significance of the sensation novel as well as looking at it in its specific cultural context.

Lyn Pykett is Senior Lecturer in English at the University of Wales in Aberystwth.

0 7463 0725 X paperback 96pp £6.99

CHRISTOPHER MARLOWE
Thomas Healy

The first study for many years to explore the whole range of Marlowe's writing, this book uses recent ideas about the relation between literature and history, popular and élite culture, and the nature of Elizabethan theatre to reassess his significance. An ideal introduction to one of the most exciting and innovative of English writers, Thomas Healy's book provides fresh insights into all of Marlowe's important works.

Thomas Healy is Senior Lecturer in English at Birkbeck College, University of London.

0 7463 0707 1 paperback 96pp £6.99

ANDREW MARVELL
Annabel Patterson

This state-of-the art guide to one of the seventeenth century's most intriguing poets examines Marvell's complex personality and beliefs and provides a compelling new perspective on his work. Annabel Patterson – one of the leading Marvell scholars – provides comprehensive introductions to Marvell's different self-representations and places his most famous poems in their original context.

Annabel Patterson is Professor of English at Yale University and author of *Marvell and the Civic Crown* (1978).

0 7463 0715 2 paperback 96pp £6.99

WILLIAM GOLDING
Kevin McCarron

This comprehensive study takes an interdisciplinary approach to the work of William Golding, placing particular emphasis on the anthropological perspective missing from most other texts on his writings. The book covers all his novels, questioning the status of *Lord of the Flies* as his most important work, and giving particular prominence to *The Inheritors, Pincher Martin, The Spire* and The Sea Trilogy. This in-depth evaluation provides many new insights into the works of one of the twentieth century's greatest writers.

Kevin McCarron is Lecturer in English at Roehampton Institute, where he teaches Modern English and American Literature. He has written widely on the work of William Golding.

0 7463 0735 7 paperback 80pp £5.99

WALTER PATER
Laurel Brake

This is the only critical study devoted to the works of Pater, an active participant in the nineteenth-century literary marketplace as an academic, journalist, critic, writer of short stories and novelist. Approaching Pater's writings from the perspective of cultural history, this book covers all his key works, both fiction and non-fiction.

Laurel Brake is Lecturer in Literature at Birkbeck College, University of London, and has written widely on Victorian literature and in particular on Pater.

0 7463 0716 0 paperback 96pp £6.99

ANGELA CARTER
Lorna Sage

Angela Carter was probable the most inventive British novelist of her generation. In this fascinating study, Lorna Sage argues that one of the reasons for Carter's enormous success is the extraordinary intelligence with which she read the cultural signs of our times – from structuralism and the study of folk tales in the 1960s – to, more recently, fairy stories and gender politics. The book explores the roots of Carter's originality and covers all her novels, as well as some short stories and non-fiction.

Lorna Sage teaches at the University of East Anglia, where she is currently Dean of the School of English and American Studies.

0 7463 0727 6 paperback 96pp £6.99